Meditations for Awakening

Larry Moen

UNITED STATES
PUBLISHING

Published by: United States Publishing
                       3485 Mercantile Avenue
                       Naples, Florida 33942

Cover Art: Charles Frizzell © "Self Portrait"

Illustrations: Patty Smith

Printed in the United States of America.

Library of Congress Cataloging-in-Publication Data

Meditations for Awakening / [edited by] Larry Moen.
        p.   cm.
    Rev. ed. of : Guided imagery, v. 3.
    ISBN 1-880698-77-3 : $11.95
    1. Meditation. 2. Imagery (Psychology) 3. Visualization.
4. Self-actualization (Psychology) I. Moen, Larry, 1948-.
II. Guided imagery.
BF637.M4G85   1994
153.3'2 — dc20   93-37569
                                      CIP

To Human Light Beings Everywhere

Let the scattered mind play.
You are not your thoughts;
you are the light.

— L.M.

Contents

Introduction

Meditations for Awakening is a collection of guided imageries to help individuals awaken to higher consciousness, and tap talents hidden within. By opening the inner frontier one will also utilize the power of visualization to improve physical and emotional health.

One is limited to past belief systems placed in the brain by society's programming. This book explores the Light and Dark side of the personality allowing acknowledgment and acceptance equally. This enables the sightful one to exist wholly in Divine Energy without fear or encumbrances of the past. It is not easy, but anything worth while seldom is. Like brushing teeth, the more it is done the less thought is involved.

The Light category which contains the goodness of God, Love and Truth is the basis for feeling. It's Dark duality contains the opposite which reflects Satan, Hate and Deceit and is the basis for emotion. Without motion matter does not exist. Motion or emotion is a vital ingredient to obtain its link with feeling. The two constantly move within themselves and are the expression of Divine Energy desiring to experience Itself.

We all have the answers within: we need only to locate the Source which for different people are manifested in numerous ways. Using outside tools as a method to tap into the Higher Self are fine as long as the individual realizes Insights or Wisdom begins and ends with that person. Some people commune with Spirit through prayer, yoga or devotional rituals. Some people think they channel outside entities, ancestors, or being from other planets, others use tools such as tarot, crystals, jewelry palm reading, astrology or runes. I know a woman that holds her right arm and fingers into the air as though she is a human antenna receiving a message from one of the above lists. No matter how ridiculous a method may seem it is acceptable as long as the communication lines are open with Higher Self.

Guided meditation or visualization is the most profound way I have discovered the link between feelings and emotions.

I believe that everything that has ever been is contained in each one of us. To analyze the ocean, only one drop of sea water is needed. And so it takes only one person's Soul to know Universal Energy. One person's Soul holds the answers to all. Every person is a Drop of that Divine Energy. And that Energy can be Felt in the body or seen visually as Light. We are drops of Light in the sea of humanity. When we embrace the Light, the Fear of human existence vanishes.

The purpose for physical existence is to use our bodies as filters to purify our Light. To work through lessons by seeing the mirror of our own Energy in everything. We have free undisturbed will to make the choice of Light, Dark, or any Shade in-between. The idea is to bring the Heavy third dimensional frequency level upward to Light.

What keeps us from reaching the depths of our Divine Energy, from experiencing the Light is the trap of our own Fear-based perceptions.

For example, by letting go of past programming one can recognize the relationship of duality in all capitalized words in this paragraph. These Perceptions of Reality are Nothing More than Our Own Thoughts Given to Us by Our Environment, Our Culture, and Our Society. Society has set the Parameters of Reality in such a Manner that It Acts as a Prison, Keeping Us All in Manageable, Predictable Situations. These Barriers Keep Us from Realizing Our Full Potential and From Experiencing Oneness as True Energy That is the Source of All Life. We Have Access to That Light Whenever We Choose. We Need Not be Victims of the Society in Which We Live. We Are Responsible to Awaken Ourselves from Sleep. It is Our Thoughts that Keep the Doors Locked and Block out the Light. Guided Meditation is the Tool I have Chosen to Transcend the Confinement of this Programming.

It is time for us to change our old patterns, to declare our freedom, and to wake up. It is important to be Oneness and experience the Light in every human being, material object, in every situation, in every part of our lives.

You may begin to realize that you can see beyond your limited desires, past this reality and into an expanded one. When you "see the Light," you realize that your consciousness is what you choose it to be. Shed your old version of consciousness and walk toward the Light, become the Light, and send the Light.

– L. M.
March 1994

How to Use This Book

If you have never practiced guided imagery or meditation, do not be concerned. Everyone has visualized to some degree, and this book offers a variety of guided imageries that can be practiced by anyone following a few simple instructions. No special classes or courses are needed. If prayer is part of your life, then you have already experienced a kind of meditation. So relax and enjoy the journey.

Types of Meditation

While traditional meditation requires a quiet unoccupied mind, guided imagery creates a scene or group of scenes developed to fulfill the purpose of the imagery. An imagery designed to help you get ahead in your career might involve climbing a mountain or finding your way on a difficult jungle path. The object of the journey is to help psychologically orient yourself for achievement, healing, relaxation, or numerous other areas of change or growth.

Where and When Should I Meditate?

These journeys can be experienced by reading them silently or out loud alone or with a partner. You may wish to tape record journeys in your own voice and play them back at times best for you. You may also wish to share these journeys with a group.

Visualization can really be done anywhere. While waiting in a doctor's office, on an airplane, during a walk, or even sitting at your desk.

However, these journeys are best practiced in a quiet place where you will not be interrupted and where you can be in a relaxed position: with eyes closed lying down, sitting in a chair, or perhaps sitting in a cross-legged manner with your back straight. Do not choose a position because you think you should; choose the one most comfortable for you.

The best time for using a guided imagery is what is best for you. Often people will use uplifting, invigorating journeys to start their days; soothing, tension relieving imageries for midday breaks; and relaxing, creative visualizations for evenings.

Group meditations are useful for promoting creativity in work projects and for encouraging people to pull together for business or community activities. An excitable, rambunctious group of children can be calmed down using imagery as well.

Pauses

Many journeys have one or more a "pauses." The length of time you take at these pauses will depend on your own experiences: it can be a few minutes or an hour. You may determine the length of the pause before you begin or during the journey.

What if I Fall Asleep?

Some people have such relaxing experiences that they believe they may have fallen asleep. Usually they have not. But to be sure, you can place one of your elbows in a upright position so that if you start to doze off, your arm will wake you up as it falls.

Music

Music can enhance the journeys, providing it is quiet and does not contain abrupt changes in tempo or pitch. The tape "Creative Imagineering" is pure ambient music, which can develop or increase visualization abilities. An order form is located at the back of this book for this and other tapes.

Breathing and Relaxation

All of the exercises contained in this book provide basic instructions for deep breathing at the beginning of each journey. Be aware that this breathing is not gasping or hyperventilation but deep, slow, controlled inhales and exhales. Most people breathe from their mid- or upper chests, but deep relaxing breath comes from "belly breathing." Inhale through your nose and expand your stomach. When you exhale, contract your stomach and gently force the air up through your lungs and out through your nose or mouth, whichever you prefer.

But What if I Can't Visualize?

Give yourself permission to visualize. Allow your mind to play and create and expand on what images you do see. Be patient with yourself. Say to yourself "If I could visualize something what would it look like."

Begin by practicing with objects that are familiar to you. Imagine a room in your home, your favorite vacation spot, or the picture of a loved one. Add movement and color to the image and allow your mind to be free and wander through the pictures you are creating. Practice this as you would anything else and soon you will be able to visualize fantastic, imaginary scenes that will stimulate and enhance your guided journeys.

Turn now to journeys in this book. Look through them and choose the ones that are best for you at this time. You may wish to begin by reading them silently to yourself, then aloud.

Enjoy these journeys, their wonderful vivid images, their life-enhancing qualities, and their ability to help you achieve your goals and desires.

Awakening

1

Creative Imagination

Guide: Joan Borysenko, Ph.D.

*"Creative imagination is similar to hypnosis;
to 'get into' it, first you must let go."*

Introduction

The notion that mental reviews of physical activities actually cause muscle movements is well accepted. Do you notice any physiological reaction to your imagination? Every time you think about something, you are imagining. The details of the process differ from person to person, but everyone has the ability to imagine. The first step is to center on breathing or to meditate for a few minutes. In the second step, you are mentally suggesting something that is different from your immediate frame of reference. Imagination is an outgrowth of meditation, the mind is guided into absorption in a directed fantasy; there is a goal. The last few minutes at the end of meditation, when the unconscious is most receptive, is the ideal time to practice creative imagination. Following is a simple exercise that you may wish to modify to suit your own situation or preferences.

The Journey

Take a deep breath, and let it go with a sigh of relief.... On each of the next few out breaths, let go a little more, letting yourself sink down.... In a moment you can count back from ten to one, continuing to let go a little more with each out breath. You can use your imagination to help you let go. With each breath, you might float a little higher in a hot air balloon, imagining the feeling of the gently swaying basket. Or you might enjoy lying on a beach, at the tide line, imagining the waves washing over you gently on the in breath and receding, taking with them any tension or dis-ease, on the out breath.... Perhaps some other image comes to mind.... So count back from ten to one in the way that suits you best....

Now imagine a beautiful sunlit day in a peaceful place. It may be someplace you know or someplace that comes to mind now.... Let your senses fill in the details. What is the earth like under you feet?... Imagine how the sun feels, soak up the warm glow, and take it deep inside, letting it energize and balance every cell.... How does the breeze feel?... What are the colors like?... Imagine all the things that make the scene beautiful. Are there sounds? Birds or wind or surf? Enjoy yourself there....

Now find a comfortable spot and settle into it.... Imagine your breathing as a stream of warm, loving energy. Direct that loving feeling into your head... your neck... your shoulders.... Breathe that feeling of warmth into your arms and hands.... Fill your heart with love and let the feeling suffuse your entire torso.... Breathe love into your belly... your pelvis.... Feel it traveling down your legs... right to the bottoms of your feet.

Now imagine yourself looking healthy and peaceful. The sunlight is shining very brightly. As you breathe in, let it

enter your body like a sunbeam through the top of your head.
With each in breath, allow the light to grow brighter and
brighter. The light is peaceful and loving. Let go to that
love.... Now sit quietly in meditation for a few minutes to
allow your unconscious mind to absorb and reflect on your
experience and then, whenever you're ready, come back and
open your eyes.

*Joan Borysenko, Ph.D., is co-founder and former director of the
Mind/Body Clinic, New England Deaconess Hospital, Harvard
Medical School. She is currently president of Mind/Body Health
Sciences Inc. which she founded with her husband, Myrin Borysenko, Ph.D. She holds a doctorate in anatomy and cellular
biology from Harvard Medical School and is one of the pioneers of
the new medical synthesis called psychoneuroimmunology.*

2

Cosmic Tree

Guide: Tom Kenyon

*"Discover the transformative power of light
as it moves throughout your body and mind."*

Introduction

In this exercise you will be using imagery to facilitate the movement of energy and awareness through your body via the central and peripheral nervous systems.

This is a very energizing visualization technique for most people. It was originally designed as part of an extensive program to boost brain performance. For best results, play soft music in the background that allows you to turn your awareness within.

Practiced on somewhat of a regular basis, this exercise will increase your awareness of the interface between your body and mind.

The Journey

Sitting comfortably, close your eyes and allow the sounds you are hearing to support you as you turn your awareness deeper inside. Be aware of your body, let your awareness be on your skin and with you awareness scan the entire outside surface of your body....

And now imagine that your body has turned into a galaxy of stars, every atom a radiant sun. Notice that most your body is filled with space, and let yourself drift comfortably through this space filled with stars and beautiful light. Let your awareness be pulled wherever it wishes to go within this vast galaxy of stars that is your body. As you drift, you may receive communications and feelings. If you feel your body wanting to communicate something to you, let yourself receive it, or there may be nothing at all, just pleasant feelings as you drift comfortably through this galaxy of stars.

Pause

Now imagine that your body is surrounded by a cocoon of the purest white light. Allow the cocoon to extend outward from the body as far as it wishes to go. This cocoon of white light seals your body of stars and its protective power. This light has the ability to heal and to transform your brain and mind, even the cells of your body.

From deep within the center of the brain, a beautiful pink light begins to pulse and radiate its energy throughout the brain. Allow yourself to feel this warm light radiating through every cell and neuron of your brain. And now the pink light begins to move down the spinal cord into the neck and throat. Feel this pink light radiating down into the throat and neck. The cocoon of white light continues to radiate its energy all around you and into the galaxy of stars that is your body. The pink light continues to move down the spinal cord, behind the lungs and the heart. Feel this beautiful pink light moving down the spinal cord behind the lungs and the heart. The pink light continues to move down the spinal cord behind the stomach and intestines. Follow the pink light as it flows down to the very base of the spine so that your entire spinal cord from the brain all the way down to your tail bone is filled with this radiant pink light floating in a galaxy of stars, surrounded by a cocoon of purest white light. And now allow the pink light from your brain and spine to radiate out through the network of nerves in your body. Let this light flow out through the thousands and thousands of branches and limbs of your nervous system. Extending like a tree into every part of your body. Feel the pink light flow into the nerve branches of your face and hands. Feel the pink light flowing into the nerve branches of your arms and hands. Feel the light flowing through your trunk and torso... down into your thighs and legs... all the way down into your feet and toes. Feel the pink light moving through your nerves into the organs and tissues, so that your body is filled with thousands upon thousands of radiant pink branches, many of which end at the skin.

Pause

Now notice your breath without changing it in any way. Just be aware of it. Notice the inhale and the exhale. And now with each inhale draw in the white light from the cocoon. Draw it into the tiny fibers of the skin and allow the white light to be drawn through the body all the way up into the spine and the brain. On the exhale, let the white light circulate through the body as it wishes. The breath need not be deep at all; just let it be natural. Feel the white light entering every nerve pathway on the inhale. Feel the white light as it is drawn through the entire body, up the spine and into the brain. With each exhale feel the white light circulating through the body. With each inhale and exhale you are cleansing and stimulating your nervous system, healing it and activating potentials beyond your imagination. The more deeply you allow yourself to feel the movement of energy and light in your nervous system, the more powerful the effects. Remember that you are in control of this experience. Feel it and experience it as deeply as you can.

Pause

Continue to draw the white light in on the inhale, through your nervous system and up into your spine and into your brain. Letting the light circulate through the body, on the exhale. Continue to focus on your breath in this way as I tell you a story.

This story is something for your conscious mind to do while your unconscious mind works to clear your brain and mind of all things no longer needed... opening your brain and mind to new potentials, new abilities, and powers.

Once upon a time, a long time ago, long enough to have been forgotten, there was a very special child, and the child's name was you. You lived in a great castle. Somehow, no one knows for sure why it happened, but the windows and doors were locked and the great castle was filled with darkness. You could not see or feel or touch or smell or taste the beautiful world outside. And you wandered for very long time inside searching for a way outside. And as the story goes, one day you came across a beautiful jewel hidden in a room that no one remembered, and holding it in your hands it pulsed a beautiful pink light out into the darkness of the great castle. A wizard appeared in its light and passed a magic wand over your head and said, "Now is the time to be transformed." The doors and the windows flew open, and a beautiful white light poured into the great castle. As you stepped outside, a dove flew down from the heavens.

Take as long as you need to return to this time. There is no rush and when you feel ready, just slowly open your eyes.

Tom Kenyon, M.A. lives in Shelton, Washington, and holds a master's degree in Psychological Counseling from Columbia Pacific University. He is the founder and director of research and development for ABR, Inc. (Acoustic Brain Research) a leader in psychoacoustic research. Psychoacoustics is the study of how sound, language, and music affect the brain and human behavior. He is also the originator of Body/Mind Re-education™ a form of rapid transformation used by therapists and counselors. Mr. Kenyon conducts human potential trainings in both the United States and Asia.

3

Deep Pool

Guide: Cayce Brooks

*"Enter the castle of your mind. Take a torch from
a bouquet of fireflowers."*

Introduction

My friend Irshya says that to truly connect with the all-that-is, I need to dive into the deep, still pool that has no bottom. By doing this of my own choice, I can lose myself (ego) and become one with the inner river of light. Because I am afraid of water on a conscious level, this a thrilling meditation to channel. My conscious self is taken through the imagery as my spirit self writes it all down. Learning to trust my spirit self and believing it is for my highest good are just two of the lessons that came through with this meditation. Personal empowerment and the ability to direct healing energy makes this, for me, my most significant meditation to date. I'm still not wild about getting in water, but now I know that deep pools and their healing energies come in many forms. Total emersion of the spirit is the point... the point of light.

The Journey

Ground and center. Enter the castle of your mind. Take a torch from a bouquet of fireflowers. The fireflower burns brightly and will not go out. You have entered at the top of a high tower. In front of you is a door. Open it and see a staircase leading down. Each step takes you deeper into your own self. There is no danger here. This is your spine you are descending. Down you step with the fireflower of your self knowledge lighting your way easily. Now you are at the bottom of the staircase and before you is another door. You reach for the handle, and it opens easily in. You walk in the room to find a pool of clean, still water. It looks like a mirror, and the light of the fireflower shows the room empty except for the calm, deep pool. You place the fireflower in a wall bracket and face the water. You know that you need to strip down to the essential you before you dive in. Take a moment to remove fears and doubt, emotional baggage, and unnecessary thoughts from the day. When you feel yourself to be light and free in spirit, return to the edge of the pool

Deep breath in and out... deep breath in and dive in. The water parts to accept you, enfolding you in its warm embrace as you kick and propel yourself deeper and deeper. Slowly release your last breath, safe in the knowledge that you can breathe this water when you need to. Deeper and deeper you go. Ahead of you is a band of light. The closer you get, the wider this light becomes. You reach it, and now you are pulled into the flow of light. You find yourself in an underground current of life force to which you willingly release all control. You are flying in this light river, flying toward the Source. The energy fills every part of your body and soul. You are now made of light, flowing easily in the current. You feel empowered, at one with all energy, and at peace with the all that is you.

You notice that you seem to be spiraling up and slowing down. Now you are floating in lazy spirals upward toward a bright light. Gently, easily, upward you float on the breath of God/Goddess toward the light that is all that you are. Now you start using your arms and legs, pulling through the energy, kicking yourself higher and higher.

Suddenly, your head and shoulders break the surface of the light, and you find yourself treading water in a beautiful, peaceful pool of water, deep in a green forest. The pool is surrounded by silent towering trees and the light in this forest is a gentle, green healing light. You swim to the edge and climb out. There is a path in front of you. You follow it to a chair made of crystal. You sit in this chair and experience the clear mind of your all-ness, be-ing. From here you can direct your thoughts and energies for any type of healing or creative endeavor. Sit and relax with this energy until....

Cayce Brooks is a poet, artist, carpenter, and mother. She tries to manifest the Divine Feminine in her life by bringing out the sacred in even the most ordinary. She practices earth magic in the mountains of north Georgia surrounded by the love and support of a wide circle of friends.

4

Full Moon

Guide: Chrystle Clae

"Face your shadow-self and cleanse negative energies and emotions from your spirit."

Introduction

"Full Moon" was inspired by a gathering of like-minded souls at the Harmonic Convergence. It provides a sense of cleansing and rejuvenation of the spirit as it allows a release of negative emotions.

The Journey

Begin by taking a few slow deep breaths.... Feel the air.... Concentrate on your breath. Breathe in slowly through the nose. Exhale rapidly through the mouth... deep slow breaths in and out.

Imagine you are seated and riding a soft, warm donkey... climbing slowly in the light of the full moon at the top of a cool mountain trail. Feel the donkey as you pat it on the cheek.... A little ahead on the winding path, your guide smiles as a signal that you're almost there. You know that you're going to a special place. You guide motions for you to dismount. As he tends to the donkeys, he directs your

13

attention to a beautiful courtyard inside the gate. As he opens it for you... in the center of this courtyard is a carefully tended roaring fire... you instinctively walk towards it and feel the warmth as you come nearer but instead of seeing the fire you seem to be standing in front of a mirror. You appear to be looking at an image of yourself... but look a little closer. You can see now that what stands before you is no mirror... you are standing face to face with the darker side of your nature... your shadow self. There is no need to fear this shadow image.

Take a good look at all the negative aspects of yourself. Realize all these aspects of yourself are brought out by fear... fear of not being loved... fear of not being accepted for the real you that's inside. You're facing all the negative aspects of yourself... your shadow... because it has agreed to be cleansed, to be washed clean here tonight... that's what the fire has been prepared for. Watch as your shadow-self willingly walks into the flames. You can still see the outline of its form as it becomes a bright red. In the red flame, it is burning up all of the selfishness, greed, arrogance, and anger that was inside you. At the same time you can feel a tingle at the base of your spine and feel the positive red spinal vibration nurturing the understanding, grounded side of your nature... leaving you with a sense of balance and enthusiasm.

As you look again into the fire, you see your shadow form take on an orange color and you feel all your doubt, pride, and imagined hurts evaporate. Within your own body a little higher on your spine (in the area of the reproductive organs), you can sense a spinal orange surge as your creative energy is stimulated... you've a new feeling of confidence in your relationships with others....

Your shadow, still in the flames, becomes a bright yellow as it burns up all your negative emotions of fear, inferiority, and over-sensitivity. In your body (in the belly button area of your spine), you feel a warming yellow spiral as it increases your own sense of personal power. You have a new clarity of your emotional, sensitive nature and a trust in your "gut feelings."

Once more your shadow changes flame color to green as it burns down the walls you've erected to protect yourself from being hurt.... Those same "protective" walls have been a barrier to allowing in the love of others. Feel a green spiral now in the heart area of your spine. Sense refreshed opening to the beauty and love in all life... feel a new sense of compassion growing inside your heart.

The untruths, deceptions, evasiveness, and manipulative side of your nature are dissolved as your shadow becomes an electric blue flame and the blue spiral enters the throat chakra area of your body. It encourages you to communicate and express your inner feelings and thoughts — to express your truth in some way.

Your shadow turns a deep blue-red color as it burns the veil that stood between the superficial world and your true inner existence. You feel the indigo spiral stimulate the area between your eyebrows, in the center of your forehead. This gentle massage allows you to hear the music that is always all around you, music that is an expression of love for your inner ears to hear and your mind's eye to observe as pulsating beautiful light.

Your shadow is becoming clearer as it turns to a violet flame tumbling down those final walls of fear, doubt, and misunderstanding. The violet spiral tingles the top of your head, and you know in the days to come, through time spent and effort given... you will understand your divine purpose... the simple reason of why you are here in a body walking the earth... you are no longer limited by the notions that others or circumstances out of your control have the ability to block you from what is important for you to accomplish. You begin to understand the uses of adversity.

The fire, the shadow, and yourself are enveloped in the clarity, the purity of the golden white light rainbow, vibration that is the result of your cleansing.

Chrystle Clae is an astrologer, psychic counselor, and teacher in Seminole, Florida. She is a nationally-known writer on the subject of metaphysics and she has a "Starlight Motivations" column in the Colorado Star Beacon *and "Daily Motivations" column in the nationally distributed* Foretold. *She is listed in* Who's Who in Service to the Earth.

5

Journey to the Stars

Guide: Mina Sirovy, Ph.D.

"An inspirational journey into innerstellar space."

Introduction

This visualization occurred during a moon meditation. It gathers much power in a group setting, although I have also used it with individual clients. Valuable messages for higher sources are accessible and can be shared when this meditation is done in a group. Similar feelings and visualizations often merge group members into harmony. The Earth needs the powerful healings that his journey can provide.

The Journey

Get comfortable and relax into receptivity, making sure you won't be interrupted. As you close your eyes and breathe deeply, your whole body settles down. Counting slowly from one to twenty, feel yourself gracefully... gradually ascending on a golden escalator. One... two... three... four... five... six... seven... eight... nine... ten... eleven... twelve... thirteen... fourteen... fifteen... sixteen... seventeen... eighteen... nineteen... twenty. Allow your breathing and your imagery to relax you. Let go... feeling lighter.

Pause

Now as you are feeling relaxed and receptive to Creative Intelligence, you are blissfully encased in a beautiful bubble. This is an iridescent bubble that protects and propels — protects and propels you up, up, up into the air. It's filled with white light of the cosmos. You look down and see the tree tops, the roof tops, the busy highways. A lovely patchwork quilt of green and yellow earth pockets is laid out underneath you, reassuring you that you'll return to familiar surroundings. As you drift up through the white fluffy, moist clouds, they disperse as your thoughts are dispersing, getting farther and farther apart.

Pause

Soon you can see the orb of the earth. It has a soft golden flow about it. You're floating up, up and away into the paths of stars and planets... your own inner stellar space. There is a faint hum reaching your ears even though you're in the bubble — like angels singing — and your surroundings are getting brighter and brighter with an intense flow of bluish white light. You feel a rush of expansiveness as you are immersed in love and light and harmony and peace. You want to stay here forever because it feels like home.

Pause

As you are hovering, you begin to see hints of gossamer wings and shadows of faces vaguely familiar. Allow yourself to encounter a guide or teacher or loved one crossed over. They have a loving message for you. Quietly listen and absorb the healing sounds and feelings coming from this source.

Pause

It has been a blissful homecoming — a holy space to which you'll return again and again for sustenance. You are so blessed, and you accept with thanks the gift of love and light you've received.

Pause

As you descend slowly through the myriad of stars and star beings, you want to share your blessing. There below you is the Earth needing your healing. As you approach the Earth, you pick a special spot to which to send healing. You project your love and light to that earthly place, envisioning wholeness and health, knowing it is gratefully received. Just as Mother Earth has nurtured you, you assume the mission of helping to bring the entire planet into higher consciousness. You continue descending, fulfilled with a sense of well-being and peace.

Pause

As you gently settle down to Earth you remember the message you have received. All around you as you touch down are your family on the material plane. They're all encased in bubbles too! As you approach each other joyfully, your bubbles all merge into one big bubble full of love and familiar laughter. All is well.

Mina Sirovy, Ph.D. has a private practice as a psychotherapist/ hypnotist in Oceanside and Fallbrook, California. She leads guided visualizations at New Thought Churches and is a newly ordained Spiritualist Minister.

6

Lagoon

Guide: Jack Kern

*"Experience gently leaving behind the old self
and being reborn into new possibility."*

Introduction

This imagery was created for an Easter Morning meditation. It is about renewal and rebirth. Too often we stay in the realm of words or thoughts, and through this meditation I want to bring the experience into a physical plane. As you do this visualization try to experience the feeling of the "old" dropping away, and new opportunities that present themselves when this happens.

There is a recognition in this meditation of the two paths — one that is difficult and requires some sacrifice. Experience is supposedly the best teacher, but is not always the comfortable way. Sometimes it is possible to choose the smoother path to inner realization.

This meditation is most effective when done slowly taking lots of time to experience and appreciate the changes.

The Journey

Allow yourself to relax and prepare to go on this journey. Imagine you and some companions are on a tropical island with a dense jungle and a beautiful blue lagoon.... A protected lagoon, protected by a barrier reef from the sea, so the water is quiet and there are no large creatures in it, nothing to threaten you. Lift up your eyes and look across at the far side of the lagoon. There is something on a hill there, something shining in the sun. You are intrigued. It seems to be drawing you toward it, and you have to find out what it is. You try to get your companions to swim the lagoon with you. Only a few do, and they kind of hang back and follow your lead.... The rest take the hard way through the dense jungle.

Pause

You begin to swim, the water is warm and supportive. You are amazed at how easy it is to swim in this lagoon. You are aware of others swimming behind you, and you are glad they are there, but you are far out ahead. As you swim, you begin to feel layers and layers of the past peel away from you, feeling as if encrustations of centuries were sloughing off. You feel the weight of old ideas and fears and habits gently break up and drop off. This is magic water in the lagoon! Your clothes disintegrate and drop away. The weight of the world drops from your shoulders. Layers of skin peel off, and fresh, new, unwrinkled and unmarked skin comes forth from underneath – skin like that of a baby. You are aware of those who chose to go through the jungle... aware that they were going through a similar process where the thorns and briars are tearing away at their clothes and old stuff. You feel for them, and you give thanks that you have chosen the lagoon.

Pause

When you reach the other side, you walk out of the water on the gently sloping bottom, and come up on the beach. There, waiting for you, are fresh new clothes... more beautiful than any you have ever had before. You put them on and walk up the hill toward the light, toward whatever was shining on the hill.

Pause

As you approach it, you see a giant crystal, with thousands of facets, reflecting the light of the sun. As you look at each facet, you see your own reflection there in the light. You see the person you have always known you were... the person you have always wanted to be... new and free and alive. You look at your beautiful body and you rejoice in its strength and youth. You feel so happy... to finally see what you have always known is there. You continue on the pathway and you find you feel very light... and you realize you are running down the path with no effort at all. You can continue now to explore the freedom of this place or you can return to this room, knowing that you may return to this lagoon anytime you wish.

Jack Kern, who calls himself a "continual seeker" has been the minister of the Unity Church in Naples, Florida, since its inception in 1968. Formerly a businessman, he has been a Unity Minister for 32 years previously serving in Boston and St. Louis.

7

Magical Personality

Guide: Wayne Dyer, Ph.D.

"You have created your own personality, and thus you have the ability to change any part of it.

Introduction

Forget for a moment that you have been taught that you cannot help having the personality that you have, that you have inherited it from your parents, or that the people cannot truly change. Forget the notion that some people have higher intelligence than others, or that talent is inherited and you were shortchanged. Let all of that go in your inner vision, and simply see yourself living and performing at the level of real magic. You must develop within you a new knowing that you have the capacity, through your invisible spiritual self, to create any change that you can conceive of for yourself. That is, if you can authentically believe in it, you can create it.... You can manifest real magic in your own inner life, and become the person you once thought was possible only for others to become.

The Journey

What would you like to be able to say about your own unique personality? Create a fantasy in your mind and imagine exactly how you would most like to be. Rather than looking

23

at what you see now, look to what you would truly like to enjoy as your personality. What level of confidence would you like to exhibit as you meet with other people in all walks of life? Would you like to be more assertive? Less inward and contemplative, or more so? More loving and gentle? More or less vulnerable? More tender? Less anxious and nervous? Create in your mind a picture of the kind of personality that would serve you best.

For now, just know that all of these inner imaginings can be translated into physical behavior, for that is precisely what you have been doing all along, ever since you showed up here in the human form that you occupy. You have been imagining yourself as more or less confident, more or less nervous, and so on. Even if you weren't aware of it, that is how your personality got shaped. You are acting upon those inner visions all the time. When you know rather than doubt that you can elect the personality that is best for fulfilling your purpose here, and you trust in your ability to be that person both in a spiritual and a physical sense, then you will create the real magic that will transform your present life. You will literally become that personality that you could only fantasize about, and you will adopt physical behaviors that will reflect your miraculous new inner vision.

Dr. Wayne Dyer is the author of numerous books including his most recent national best seller, Real Magic. *Dr. Dyer is a psychotherapist with a doctorate in counseling psychology. He lectures across the country to groups numbering in the thousands and appears regularly on radio and television. Dr. Dyer lives with his family in southern Florida.*

From Real Magic *by Dr. Wayne W. Dyer, copyright © 1992. Reprinted by permission of Harper Collins Publishers.*

8

Mountain Peaks

Guide: Annette Covatta

"Beyond mountains, more mountains."
— Haitian Proverb

Introduction

Mountains evoke a sense of expansiveness. This imagery can stretch the consciousness, open the heart to messages, and offer clarity and insight in the face of ambiguities. Your own inner guide will let you know when and how often to use this meditation, but usually it helps with feelings of a diminishing life or when you have reached a plateau.

The Journey

Take some moments to unwind.... Find a comfortable posture for your body.... Let your body be comfortable, yet alert.... Let the busy, swirling thoughts you are carrying inside you drop away.... Feel a relaxation move through your body.

Bring your attention, now, to the movement of your breath... the never-ending, life-giving flow of your breath. Bring all of your awareness to the rhythm of your breath... inhale... exhale... in and out....

As you inhale, I want you to tense your forehead, contracting the muscles as tightly as you can. Hold the breath and the tension for a slow count of three. One... two... three.... Then, release the breath and your forehead into relaxation. Now, do the same with your eyes... your mouth and jaw... neck and shoulders... arms and hands... torso... legs... feet....

You are completely relaxed now... totally present to this moment... this place. You have nothing else to do, to think, but to *be*... to be *here* now.

Come with me now into a valley... a meadow... where the ground is soft with green grass. Feel the grass under your feet. Enjoy the greenness and the smell of it. As you look up and around you, you are dazzled by the majesty of lofty mountains encircling the valley. Several peaks are covered with white snow.

You notice a trail just ahead that seems to wind its way up the mountain. You follow the path. The trail climbs steeply, then levels off for a bit — a welcomed relief of plateau. You keep moving, taking in the wonderful surprises of foliage and rocks along the way.

The delicate flowers in a variety of soft colors, nestled in the crevices of the rocks, make you smile. They are untouched in their pure, natural state, growing simply as they are supposed to, without being cultivated or domesticated. Wild flowers. Just being natural. Natural, ordinary beauty... you ask yourself, "What, in my life, has this quality of ordinary, natural beauty?"

Along the way, you notice uncharted terrains yet to be explored. The wilderness.... Perhaps, someday, someone will venture off the clear path, opening to the possibility of discovering new wonders, — fresh miracles of nature... taking the risk of getting lost or slipping on loose rocks.... You ask yourself, "When, in my life, have I taken risks? Does fear hold me back from taking chances? Do I think of myself as a risk-taker?" You ponder these things gently, quietly, as you decide to move on.

You reach the peak... astounded by the vista of rolling hills far away, meeting the hovering clouds. In the valleys below, you notice patches of colors — green, brown, yellow, and auburn. The rarified air deepens the silence.

You look around you where you are standing. You notice small rocks idly clustered near your feet. You are drawn to one stone in particular. You pick it up. You feel connected to it. You start exploring it. Using all your senses, you notice its color and shape, the feel of its texture.... It's as if this stone at the mountain peak had been waiting for you. You sense its consciousness. Looking about you, stretching your gaze into the beyond, you sense the consciousness of these mountains. And now you sense that this stone... these mountains... are part of *your* consciousness. You feel the connection... the communion... the oneness.

Rest here awhile.... Feel the flow of energy between you and your stone. You might want to ask the stone if it has a message for you. Ask. Wait without pressing for an answer.... And now, feel the flow of energy between you and the mountains.... As your drink in the vastness of the mountains enveloping you, you remember the Haitian proverb: "Beyond mountains, more mountains."

It is time, now, to descend the mountain. You take a different passageway down. You reach the valley more quickly than expected. As you look about you and gaze upward to the mountain peaks, you remember the words of the Eastern philosopher, Suzuki: "Peaks and valleys... either will do."

When you feel ready, open your eyes and return to the room.

Annette Covatta, D.M.A., has a lifetime involvement in the arts and personal growth programs, and she holds a Doctor of Musical Arts from Boston University. Ms. Covatta is the founder and director of FULCRUM, an organization whose mission is to enable persons to reach their potential through the body/mind/spirit/soul connection. Through FULCRUM, she presents workshops which reflect her interest in the creative process and holistic spirituality.

9

Observer Self

Guide: Jacquelyn Small

*"The observer self is the key to transformation
for it enables consciousness to work."*

Introduction

Use this exercise when you feel it is important for [you or]
the person you're working with to get outside of their [your]
emotional reaction to a situation and see it from a wider
point of view (from the standpoint of Reality rather than
from the personal reality).

In processing this experience, pay special attention to the
difference in how the person you are guiding felt from above
as compared to being totally involved down below. Point out
that the uninvolved (higher) Self has the most loving responses. (Often we confuse passionate emotional involvement — that we feel when we are attached and needy — with
love).

Ask your client or friend to close her eyes and picture herself
totally involved in an emotional scene that is representative
of some current problem. After she has gone inward and
become silent, and you sense she is picturing the scene, guide
her with these types of statements, spoken quietly and
unobtrusively.

The Journey

Be aware of how you are feeling as you involve yourself in this scene.... Notice the look on your face and on the faces of those involved with you.... Be aware of the kind of energy that is in the air as you involve in this.... Notice your body movements.... Be aware of the intentions of yourself and others involved... the message you're trying to get across to the other(s).... Now, just feel for a moment the very essence of this experience, as though it's happening right now.... Just be with that for a while.... (Put on some quiet meditative music at this point, if possible.)

Pause

Now, rise above yourself.... All the way up into the sky... look down on the scene you left behind and see it in its entirety.... Notice what you are doing.... Notice how the other(s) are reacting to you.... Be aware of the context within which this scene is occurring... the role you and the others are playing out, the place it's happening... this particular time in history... in the city where you live... this culture... this age....

Pause

Now, very slowly allow yourself to descend back into the scene you've been witnessing.... Reenter your body and begin acting out this scene based on what you saw from above.... Notice any changes you are making in how you are relating to this situation.... Notice any changes in others.... Be aware of how your body now looks and feels.... Be aware of any insights into the situation you are having.... Be especially aware of the needs the other(s) have, or what is motivating their behavior, and notice your reactions to them now....

Pause

Allow this scene to come to an end in whatever way you wish to resolve the matter for now....

Slowly open your eyes and come back here with me.

Jacquelyn Small, M.S.S.W., author of Becoming Naturally Therapeutic *and* Awakening in Time, *has touched the lives of thousands in the innovative workshops and lectures she conducts throughout the U.S. and Canada. She currently serves on the advisory board for the national Council on Codependence. Her company, Eupsychia Inc. is a healing and training center dedicated to bridging traditional and transformational psychologies.*

10

Opening Energy Centers

Guide: Shakti Gawain

*"Every moment of your life is infinitely creative
and the universe is endlessly bountiful."*

Introduction

This is a meditation for healing and purifying your body and
for getting your energy flowing. It is an excellent one to do
in the morning when you first wake up, at the beginning of
any meditation period, or anytime you want to be relaxed
and refreshed.

When you finish this meditation you will be deeply relaxed,
yet energized and exhilarated.

The Journey

Lie down on your back with arms at your sides or with hands
clasped on your stomach. Close your eyes, relax and breathe
gently, deeply and slowly.

Imagine that there is a glowing sphere of golden light
surrounding the top of your head. Breathe deeply and slowly
in and out five times while you keep your attention on the
sphere of light, feeling it radiate from the top of your head.

Now allow your attention to move down to your throat. Again imagine a golden sphere of light emanating from your throat area. Breathe slowly in and out five times with your attention on this light.

Allow your attention to move down to the center of your chest. Once again imagine the golden light, radiating from the center of your chest. Again take five deep breaths, as you feel the energy expanding more and more.

Next put your attention on your solar plexus; visualize the sphere of golden light all around your midsection. Breathe into it slowly, five times.

Now visualize the light glowing in and around your pelvic area. Again take five deep breaths, feeling the light energy radiating and expanding.

Finally, visualize the glowing sphere of light around your feet and breathe into it five more times.

Now imagine all six of the spheres of light glowing at once so that your body is like a strand of jewels, radiating energy.

Breathe deeply, and as you exhale, imagine energy flowing down along the outside of the left side of your body from the top of your head to your feet. As you inhale, imagine it flowing up along the right side of your body to the top of your head. Circulate it around your body this way three times.

Then visualize the flow of energy going from the top of your head down along the front of your body to your feet as you slowly exhale. As you inhale, feel it flow up along the back of your body to the top of your head. Circulate the flow in this direction three times.

Now imagine that the energy is gathering at your feet, and let it flow slowly up through the center of your body from your feet to your head, radiating from the top of your head like a fountain of light, then flowing back down the outside of your body to your feet. Repeat this several times, or as long as you wish.

Shakti Gawain, author of the bestsellers Creative Visualization *and* Living in the Light, *gives clear explanations and practical guidance for anyone who desires to develop their intuition and learn to follow it, using their creative abilities to the fullest.*

Excepted from Creative Visualization, © *1978 Reprinted with permission of New World Library, San Rafael, CA 94903.*

11

Scrim

Guide: Christopher S. Rubel, Rel. D.

"A guided imagery skill developer for Seeing Through."

Introduction

The purpose of this guided imagery is to help you realize alternatives to what you are experiencing. Gradually, you will learn to penetrate the limits of your perceptions. It is possible to generalize what you are learning in this exercise to other senses, such as touch, smell, and even the sensations of your own emotions. This imagery will serve to help open you to the possibilities of softened boundaries. We are trained to see surfaces and forms. It takes opening to imagination, to alternate perceptions, if we are to see through to parallel realities, to alternative "virtual realities." You will feel open to other feelings, views, and your creativity will be enhanced immeasurably by tending to this imagery on a regular basis, say, at least once every other day.

The Journey

Choose a safe, comfortable, even pleasant environment. Find a seated or yoga-type position that suits you well. You may change positions to make yourself more comfortable at any time in this next few minutes. Allow yourself to become more comfortable. As with all relaxation, begin to concentrate on your breathing. Develop the concept of a breathing circuit, breathing in through your nose and out through your mouth. While you are doing this, inhale, raising your arms slowly. Exhale, lowering your arms to hang limp at your sides. Inhaling, spread your chest by raising your arms, breathing all the way, down deeply, diaphragm breathing, not chest breathing, relaxing, now breathing out, letting your head fall gently forward as your lungs empty. Repeat, as long as you like, for about ten to fifteen times, until you are genuinely ready to close your eyes. Slowly, let relaxation move up through your entire body.

Pause

When you recognize yourself to be more comfortable and quieter than when you began, begin to let yourself move to an inner, safe, beautiful place. This may be an imaginary place or, perhaps, some place you have enjoyed in your memory. Let it come to you. Simply ask the inner "guides" to take you to a quiet, secure place, where you may continue in this meditative imagery experience. Stay in this place, wherever it is, until you feel the sensations of being there. Feel the soft breezes, the smells, the sensations of the room, if you are inside, and let your mind detach from all disturbances that would dull or distract you from this personal safe place. Remember, this is your place. Nothing can happen here without your permission or desire, unless it is ultimately very good for you, leading you to an expanded awareness, beyond limiting boundaries that are hold you back, perhaps imprisoning you, blinding you. This is a place of gentle revelation and subtle life changes, where the opaque becomes transparent.

Pause

Come with me, now. Follow these words and let your perceptions and senses open. I want you to see a book. Look at this book and, now, as it is in focus, see beyond the cover. Without opening it, "see" its pages with printed images, letters, index, the chapter headings, as they come to your mind's eye. You have not opened this book, but you can for this moment see one page, then another, letting the pages turn. You are not reading, just seeing impressions of printed words on those pages.

Moving, now, beyond the book, you are able to see the surface under the book, upon which the book is resting. You can see the surface in your mind's eye. It is any surface that would support this book. See it, feel it with imaginary fingers, and you will detect sensations in your finger tips. Is it rough or smooth? Is it leather, wood, metal, stone, or, just what kind of surface is this upon which book is resting?

Now, lifting your eyes, you see a window above the book. There is a soft, openly woven, curtain covering this window. The bright light in the room illuminates the curtain so that you are able to see the stitching, the design, the patterns on the curtain. You see the fabric of this curtain and it becomes more and more vivid to you as you let the image become enriched. See it. See the detail of the fabric that is coming to you, that vivid pattern of stitching and design.

Somehow, as you are noticing this curtain, you begin to notice the light in the room is becoming dim, dim, dimmer, and the light outside the window is becoming brighter and brighter. You are aware of seeing through the curtain, now, almost as though it is not there. The light beyond the window illuminates a landscape, a city, a valley, mountains, or whatever comes to you beyond the window's boundary. The curtain is completely transparent, now, and you see beyond, into the next reality.

Noticing there are various aspects of this parallel dimension, this next reality, that are becoming more vivid, standing out, in a way, drawing your attention. Just follow the images and "watch" how they develop as you attend to them. Don't hesitate to let them develop from very subtle forms. You may see a tree in the field and a faucet under the tree. Then you notice the hose coming from the faucet and you follow the hose with your eye and it comes to an edge of a hole in the ground, where a gopher has dug, and the water is running down that hole. As you improve in your skill with this, you will be able to follow the water down the hole into a cave, a wonderful cave, with crystal stalagmites and shimmering stalactites. Allow and permit the images to unfold. They may be as simple or as complex as you like. When the images have developed well, let your imaginary fingers touch them, feel their surfaces, and become familiar with textures, temperatures of what you are sensing, perceiving.

Pause

We are not quite through. One more step is coming up, which is the climax of this imagery. Allowing yourself, now to see a figure in this reality beyond your room, curtain, and window. Notice this figure. You let a temporary telescope begin to bring this figure closer and closer. The image is becoming clearer and clearer, now. You see the person or animal clearly, now. The telescope is unnecessary. As soon as the figure is clear, you notice you are able to perceive illumination that seems to come from within and around the figure, and you sense a spiritual presence, a healing presence, an integrative presence in this figure that have nothing to do with the boundaries of the figure. It is as though you are seeing the created essence of this figure. As you do this, you are feeling your own essence more than at any other time. You experience your own depth, beyond all appearances and boundaries. You feel now at one with essences and realities beyond the opaque perceptions you have had previously.

This moment will deepen and become increasingly detailed, each time you let the light brighten beyond the scrim, beyond that marvelous curtain. You are in perceptual kindergarten. Know that you are beginning to see into parallel realities, perceiving through those previous limits into molecular structures, spheres of planetary systems previously unknown. And you know how weird this is, but you have no judgments or skepticism. You are able to see the eternal in someone in your life, now. You are able to be open to possibilities in others, yourself, and relationships that were diminished before this. You intend to remain open to these new dimensions and penetrations beyond your previous limits, so they will develop and mature. Allow the images to play with you. Permit them to give their gifts to you.

Pause

Gradually, now, the light beyond the curtain is fading and the light in your room is becoming brighter, to a pleasant level of illumination. The transparency of the curtain decreases as the light changes. Let yourself come to the staging place of seeing the curtain, its pattern, stitching, texture, and begin to see the book on its surface. Let all of this develop each time in its own marvelous, almost miraculous way.

You are moving back into your present time, and are letting yourself feel the strength come back into your body. Your attention is coming back to present time and space. You now have a sense of the other realities that are accompanying you and all of us each moment of our lives. It is an easy awareness, not complicated or troublesome in any way. It is just resting on your conscious mind, now, letting you know of the otherness in your life, no matter what and who you think and thought you were or are. You have moved beyond all boundaries and roles into essences that will become richer and more nourishing, more expansive each time you do this. Even the boundaries between your waking life and your dreaming life will soften. You will find your dreams becoming more available, more interesting and helpful, as a contiguous benefit of this imagery.

Thank you for entertaining this gift of softened boundaries, parallel, virtual realities, long enough to let it deepen within you. May it go with you and enhance every perception, every sensation, every idea, every act throughout the hours ahead of you, today tonight, and tomorrow. Remember, what you are perceiving is completely contingent upon conditioning and depends upon the illumination being on your side of the forms and surfaces. Remember, we choose our realities and there are other, parallel realities eclipsed by innumerable variables, in our midst right this second. One teacher, a man aware of parallel realities, said, "Lo, I am with you always." We need our boundaries, but sometimes they imprison or limit us profoundly. Let them soften, where and when you are feeling confined or too contained.

Christopher S. Rubel, has a Doctor of Religion degree in Pastoral Psychology, from S.T.C., Claremont, and an A.B. degree from Redlands University. He has been licensed as a psychotherapist since 1967 and practices in Claremont, California. He is also a Priest of the Episcopal Church and thinks of his work as "soul work."

12

Third Step

Guide: Margot Escott, M.S.W.

"Learning to make conscious contact with a higher power is one of the many free gifts offered in 12-step programs."

Introduction

In my own personal recovery and in working with others in various stages of recovery from addictions and compulsive patterns, the idea of surrendering our will to a higher power is often difficult at first. By giving ourselves permission to create a loving, compassionate higher power in our lives we are able to truly begin loving ourselves as children of God.

We are going to do a healing meditation... a guided imagery journey to help you make contact with your higher power. Give at least thirty to forty-five minutes to yourself and going to a place where you won't be disturbed. This is a time for you... a time to nurture, revitalize, and become aware of the divine love that is in you and all around you. In this meditation there will be references to a higher power. You may choose to call your higher power God or Buddha or Christ — any word that feels comfortable for you or no word at all.

The Journey

Go to that place, that deep place inside where you know all the answers and where you are pure love. Begin by taking some deep breaths in through the nose and out through the mouth. If you have some feelings right now, remember feelings are neither good nor bad, they just are. Perhaps you can imagine that you're taking your feelings and putting them into a ball of light. Take that ball of light and place it inside a box. Know that you can take back all of your feelings whenever you want them, but for now you're letting your feelings go. Do the same with all of your wonderful thoughts... bundle them up into a ball of light and take the ball of light and attach it to a string tied to a balloon. See the balloon lifting up, up, up, into the sky — taking away all of your thoughts and allowing yourself to just be here with your breath and calmness. As you breathe in, say to yourself "I am" and on the exhalation say, "At peace." Using your own breath to guide you, begin to let every cell of your body drift into a pleasant state of relaxation. Imagine all of the muscles, all of the organs, every aspect of your body totally relaxing so that you feel that you have no body. You are drifting into a beautiful state of rest, repose, and relaxation. Use your breath to bring you to calmness... breathing in the spirit of love and breathing out stress and worry.

Pause

Focus on the area around your heart and imagine a beautiful color, a healing color massaging that wonderful organ that is your heart. Bathing your heart in love and rest. As this light massages your heart, it also massages away any resentments, fears, and self-judgments that break through the walls that sometimes prevent you from truly loving yourself... the child of God that you are. Feel your heart opening and begin to feel and see a beautiful clear white light coming from your heart surrounding the energy field of your whole body, almost as if your body was enveloped in a cocoon of clear white light filled with love and compassion. See and feel your body bathed in the light of love and self-acceptance. Begin to see the light filling up the room you're in right now, so that every part of the room is filled with light. The light becomes more expansive and covers the building you are in, and it covers your community. Spreading over your state, the light continues to grow and expand as your heart energy grows and expands, bathing the entire planet earth with a healing, radiating light.

Pause

You may want to let yourself drift into an even deeper state of serenity and calmness as you become aware of a source of light coming towards you. As this light draws nearer it may or may not take the form of a being — a being that represents your higher power. It may remain as a source of light or become any form that feels right for you. If your vision has imagined a form, look into the eyes of this being and see yourself reflected in its eyes. See how they regard you with such love and compassion. Know that this is your source of truly unconditional positive love. As the light and love radiate from this being, feel it coming into your being. Feel your heart and spirit fill with the love that has always been there for you. As you allow yourself to feel love, know that you are a channel of love.

Deep in your heart hear the words of this prayer. "God I offer myself to Thee, to build with me and to do with me as Thou will. Relieve me of the bondage of self, that I may better do Thy will. Take away my difficulties that victory over them may bear witness to those I would help of Thy Power, Thy

Love, and Thy Way of life. May I do Thy will, always.

"Thy will not mine be done.

"Lord make me a channel of thy peace;
That where there is hatred I may bring love;
That where there is injury I may bring healing;
That where there is darkness I may bring light;
That where there is despair I may bring hope;
That where there is sadness I may bring joy.
Lord, grant that I may seek rather to comfort than to be comforted;
To understand rather than be understood;
To love, than to be loved.
For it is by self-forgetting that one finds;
It is by forgiving that one is forgiven;
It is in dying to self that we are born to eternal life.
They will not mine be done. Amen."

Pause

Allow yourself to affirm yourself — a child of God and a unique and precious gift. Be aware that there has never been and never will be anyone else like you — go in peace and love and allow your light to shine.

Margot Escott, M.S.W. is a social worker in private practice in Naples, Florida, where she uses visualization and guided imagery for stress management, pain control, and recovery from addictive illnesses. In 1992 she received a national grant from The Humor Project for her work on the Humor Cart at Naples Community Hospital. She presents workshops throughout the United States on "Healing with Humor and Play," "Discovering Your Inner Child," and "Visualization for Success."

13

Treasures from the Sea

Guide: Nancy Harn-Wagner

"This has been written to help you recognize and use the symbology in the life about you."

Introduction

Water is very revitalizing, and this visualization is helpful for creative energy. It also contains many healing aspects. It has been used very effectively in my medicine shield making classes because the items that appear in the path can become part of the shields. I developed this meditation while enjoying some quiet moments on the beach of the Gulf of Mexico.

The Journey

Set your mind in nature... close your eyes and see yourself by the seashore.

Breathe in the healing, salty spray of mist... long deep passages of refreshing air slowly filling your body with the breath of life... exhaling all negativity from your body. Enjoy this exhilaration until your body reaches a state of relaxed rhythmic breathing, and you feel yourself within the harmony of the earth.

45

Pause

At this time see a white light within yourself — watch it expand through your entire body and flow to all your surroundings. Know that this white light comes from your inner self and that you have totally protected yourself from any negative thoughts.

With your bare feet, touch the coolness of the Earth Mother's surface — her sandy encouragement to connect. Invite the grains to sift through your fingers and toes. Allow the moist sand to heal your body as it covers the surface of your skin, extracting long buried thoughts and inhibitions and guilt from the very basis of your soul. Take time to enjoy this transforming process as you listen to the music of nature all around you.

Hear the sea birds calling to each other in their own language and acknowledge the world that is theirs as they soar and drift with their wings fluttering and calling the spirits from above to you. Feel the wind blowing across the cool waters refreshing you with inspiration; listen with awe to the wispy sounds of gentle breezes passing by you and through you... sense the angel wings lifting your spirits while removing any sadness, distrust, or hostility you may have. Take time to enjoy this exhilaration and feel your body become lighter.

During this moment of peacefulness look out over the horizon and remember the times of the past — lives before, which are still a part of you. While standing at the water's edge, look back into your past and bring forward any hurts or differences you may have forgotten. Take a few minutes to accept the feelings, then release and allow these thoughts to be washed out to the depths of the ocean again. Forgive anyone who may have hurt you and ask forgiveness from those you may have hurt. Recognize the cool blue water as the peacefulness which you desire; notice the whiteness of foam and the churning of deep water as it represents the cleansed and purified time of your existence on earth.

As you walk farther towards the water, ask for a cleansing of heart and spirit. Step into the relaxing water and feel the healing as you go deeper into the ocean. Sink into deep beauty as pureness of soul is recognized... feel yourself swim beneath the water — notice the sea creatures as they accept your presence and begin to swim with you, inviting you to their quiet world in the depths beneath the sea.

At this time you know you have felt the presence of the Spirit, and it has become a part of you. Your body swims freely, and you are able to breathe in the water as the sea creatures do... you have reached another reality. Relax for awhile in this world of quiet tranquility.

Pause

You rise to reach the surface, knowing that cleansing has taken place.... And as the grains of sand are washed from your body, look towards the heavens and see the sun shining much brighter than before. While you lie on your back in the water floating in time and space... look up towards the white clouds high in the blue sky above and know that the soft puffs drifting above you represent moments of happiness coming into your life, for there is an endless number of clouds for your rejoicement.

Now begin to walk leisurely along the shore, taking in sights, sounds, and feelings you have experienced. As you wander aimlessly without restrictions of time or destination, choose three objects from the many that may appear along your path. These may be symbols from nature placed there for you to find in the form of shells, driftwood, leaves, seed pods, or feathers. When you have gathered the three treasures from the earth, return to your original spot next to the seashore. Place these three objects on the sand before you. Know that they are symbolic.

Pick up the three treasures one at a time, thank the Earth Mother for her gift, and ask what message is here for you. The first object you found may represent a question you wish to have answered. Hold the object in your hands and ask the question. Release the question to the winds. Allow a moment's time to pass. When you have sent the question up to the Spirit above, hold the second object in your hands and ask for a way for the answer to be manifested. Allow the Spirit to speak to you. When you feel that the time is right, place the third object in your hands and wait for the answer to come to you. Ask for a specific answer to come to you in a way you can understand. Know that this is the Spirit of the Earth coming to you. Thank the Spirit for this guidance.

Pause

As you ponder the insight you have just received, look out over the water to see a beautiful sight. A gentle dolphin has felt your presence and has appeared to you, sliding gracefully and happily through the waves, encouraging you to join her in frolic and playfulness in the sunshine. As you listen, she tells you to take time to be a child again and to enjoy the simple things offered you in life. You realize that during this time you have not been alone, your thoughts have been heard by the Spirit above and the dolphin has appeared so you may acknowledge your connection with nature and the Spirit.

And so comes the end of your journey to the seashore. Know that you have been blessed. You are welcome to visit this spot anytime you wish.

Open your eyes and be thankful for this bountiful time in nature by the sea.

Nancy Harn-Wagner is a professional visionary artist and writer who resides in Clearwater, Florida.

14

White Light Protection

Guide: Rodney L. Goulet, C.Ht.

*"It symbolizes the strongest force
in the universe, that of love."*

Introduction

This meditation was written to visualize the Divine presence as white light, invoking it to protect and heal ourselves or our loved ones from physical, psychic or relationship challenges.

The Journey

Sit or lie comfortably now. It is necessary to relax your body, in order to relax your mind. It is best to not feel discomfiture, so sit or lie with your spine straight, your feet flat on the floor, if sitting, and your hands limply on your thighs. It is important to be so comfortable that you are totally unaware of your body.

Now, take a deep breath.... Hold it for a moment... and then let it all out, see all the tension leave you now as a fine grey mist. Take a second deep breath... hold it for a moment... and let it all out, all out, see and feel the tension going. Take a last and final deep breath... hold it... and let it all out, all tension gone now, relaxed.

See in your mind's eye a white light moving towards you. It moves over and around you, encompassing you completely. Your body continues to let go and relaxes. From the tips of your toes, to the top of your head you feel a wave of white light relaxing you. Every muscles and nerve in your body is letting go, letting go, relaxing now. Your toes tingle, your calf muscles become limp, loose and relaxed. Your thigh muscles let go, moving up, your hip muscles relax, letting go. Your stomach muscles let go, your solar plexus, the center of nervous energy, lets go now. Your chest and back muscles let go, those heavy muscles that work so hard, become loose, limp and lazy. Your arms begin to relax. They are light, floating now. Your finger tips tingle with the release of tension. Your neck muscles and shoulder muscles sag loosely now, barely able to hold your head straight. Your mind is clearing now. Your forehead and cheeks relax. Every wrinkle in them smooths out. Relaxed, your jaw muscles sag, and your mouth opens slightly.

You are surrounded by White Light. There is a shield of White Light surrounding you, protecting you. It glows with love of God. As you accept the White Light into your Inner Self you know you are a source of Love. This White Light symbolizes both the love of God for you and your love of God for others. It protects you from harm at all times. It symbolizes the strongest force in all the universe, that of love. this white Light protects you from all harm, from all invasions of outside influences, and forms a wall of protective love around you. It is your armor. See now, this bright, shining, white armor protecting you. You have become a source of love and you have but to repeat these words. "I accept the White Light of Protection." And the protection occurs. Now it will spring into action covering you with an armor of love... covering you with the light of purity... covering you with protection. Whenever you say, "I accept the White Light of Protection," you are protected by God. Now visualize your loved ones, see them in your mind's eye. Now surround all those whom you love and wish to protect with the same White Light that surrounds you. You are protecting them from harm at all times. It is the mightiest force in all the universe, that of the Love of god. It forms an invisible wall of protection, it is an armor against all negativity. See White Light now encompassing and protecting your loved ones.

Now hold in your imagination and visualize that person that you wish to heal. Whether you wish to heal that person or protect yourself from them. Now surround them with White Light. See a glow of white light encompassing them. The Light that is the Love of God. This White Light cancels all negativity emanating from inside or out, protecting, healing and showing our oneness. This relationship is now healed of any apparent negativity. The Love of God now shines through. Only love remains. Send love, love is received. Only one party to a relationship is necessary for healing. Now forgive that person. Now forgive yourself and thereby heal. The shield of White Light now protects them as well as it protects you.

Now, slowly, calmly, easily begin to return to awareness. You feel perfect in every way, physically, mentally and emotionally. Every muscle and nerve in your body is loose, limp and relaxed. Your eyes feel refreshed, as though washed in sparkling, cool spring water. Open your eyes, knowing you are protected, healed and loved.

Rod Goulet attended St. Thomas College, St. Paul, Minnesota and is a graduate of the New Seminary, New York, New York where he earned a degree in Spiritual Counseling.

Gifts & Love

15

Butterflies

Guide: Larry Moen

"Be of little substance and become the Light."

Introduction

The body is the whole physical structure and substance of a human being — the flesh or material substance as opposed to the soul. To be "of substance" is to be fully conscious of your physical body. To be "of little substance" is to leave behind all consciousness of your body focusing on inner awareness. It is to give yourself permission to explore the deeper meaning of existence and to experience the Nothingness. One way of doing this is to use visualization to experience the transition from physical awareness to absorption in the Light. This guided imagery will help you move towards higher levels of existence.

The Journey

Close your eyelids, look up into the darkness, back a little and inhale deeply.... As you exhale, allow your eyes to gently roll down to their normal position.... Inhale again... and exhale, relaxing completely....

If you have any feelings or sensations in your physical body, just allow them to happen. Recognize them. Accept them and watch them leave. Inhale... and exhale....

Now begin to be aware of the outside light that is filtering through your eyelids and focus this light into your chest. Imagine exposing your chest area to the sun; feel its warmth against your skin and feel it penetrating your skin as it is absorbed into your heart center.... Now imagine that a small candle flame is burning warmly, within your spiritual heart expanding more and more and enlarging with every breath.

Pause

As the breath expands let it fill your body with light, as you focus your attention on your chest. Now feel butterflies of light exploding from your center outward.... Visualize several angel-like butterflies fluttering around your body. As you watch the transparent white butterflies quivering around your being, notice that more and more are sent out from this white light center core that you opened. Watch them as they swarm around your body, giving your body gentle kisses of love and light.

Pause

As each kiss against your skin is received from the transparent, lighted butterflies, you find that you are being energized. They help you fill your entire body with white light, and you are now consumed totally in white, radiant light. Watch the butterflies dart in and out of you as they pick up any pieces of dark, shadowy negativity and fly away with them to the sun where they are burned and transformed into pure energy. Feel the butterflies expressing all the love you desire.

Pause

It is now time to come back into conscious awareness. Allow your butterflies of light and love to fly back into your beautiful heart center and know that you can call them from this light source at any time.

The light comes directly from you as it does from everyone. One direct line from you... for you. The light of love.

Now begin to feel your toes and your feet and your legs, your stomach and back, chest and head, arms and hands. Inhale a deep cleansing breath... and with your exhalation become more and more awake.... Inhale again and stretch as you exhale. If you like, yawn as you stretch, and when you are ready open your eyes and find yourself wide awake.

Larry Moen is the editor and driving force behind the Meditations *series. As a Vietnam veteran, Mr. Moen has been aware that significant emotional events can influence one's life. Mr. Moen discovered that past programming from childhood forward can be healed and transformed using the powers of guided meditation. Subsequently, Mr. Moen embarked on an intensive study of guided visualization which he incorporates in his work with T'ai Chi, yoga and self-hypnosis. He currently leads meditation groups and speaks at seminars.*

16

Giving Is Receiving

Guide: Douglas Bloch

"Whenever you put another first, the universe puts you first."

Introduction

The law of giving flows from this truth: rather than being a fixed entity, the universe is a dynamic, flowing moving stream of energy. When you give of yourself unconditionally, you create a temporary imbalance that must be corrected. Like the molecules of air rushing in to fill a vacuum, the universe strives to replace the good you have given out.

Often, the flow will come back from a totally unexpected source. For example, you may spend a day helping Anne move into her new home. Six months later when it is your turn to move, Anne may be unavailable to help you, but Jesse calls and offers his assistance. A year later, Jesse receives some much-needed support from Bob. Like the angels of Jacob's ladder, we are one interconnected spiritual chain, reaching up to a higher ground.

There are many ways to give. You can give of your time, your money, your talents, or yourself. There are many people to whom you can give — your family, friends, or those in the human family whom you do not know. It doesn't matter how you do it; the principle is the same. Every time you extend yourself outward, the universe extends itself to you. The more you give, the more you receive.

Strive to reach out and take the hand of the soul next to you. As you extend yourself in love, you will be uplifted to a new state of joyful awareness.

The Journey

1. The more I give to others, the more the universe gives to me.
2. There is enough to go around for everyone, including me.
3. Divine love in me blesses all that I am, all that I give, and all that I receive.
4. My cup runs over. I have more than I need, and so I share with my world.
5. Every dollar I contribute to others comes back to me multiplied.
6. Create your own affirmation.

Douglas Bloch, author, counselor, and teacher, received his master's in counseling psychology from the University of Oregon. As a counselor for seventeen years, he has conducted numerous workshops and seminars on the subject of affirmations and spiritual development. He is currently a trainer for Omega Seminars and the host of his own radio program in Portland, Oregon.

17

Internal Mother

Guide: Larry Moen

"Your Internal Mother offers you eternal love and affection."

Introduction

Emotions of aloneness, depression, or rejection are traditionally healed by a mother's warm touch or words of support. A mother represents a safe place, a nurturing presence, a calm and loving sanctuary. To practice this meditation you do not have to have had an ideal relationship with your real mother. Perhaps you never knew your mother. Perhaps she had difficulties of her own and could not be the supportive, loving person you wanted her to be. Whatever your relationship is or was with your mother, send her loving energy and release her now as you begin this meditation.

Imagine now what you would like a mother to be and know that you have those qualities within you. This guided meditation will help you access those emotions.

The Journey

As you inhale bring your awareness to your feet, ankles and toes.... Exhale allowing them to drift and become heavy, heavy and limp, and just let them go.... Now inhale bringing your awareness to your calves, knees, and thighs.... Exhale allowing them to drift and become heavy, and limp. Just let them go.... Now bring your awareness to your buttocks, hips and pelvic area.... Allow them to drift and become heavy, and limp, and just let them go.... Now bring your awareness to your back, abdomen, and chest.... Allow them to drift and become heavy, heavy and limp, and just let them go.... Now bring your awareness to your shoulders, arms and hands.... Allow them to drift and become heavy, heavy and limp, and just let them go.... Now bring your awareness to your neck, head and face.... Allow them to drift and become heavy, heavy and limp, and just let them go....

Now inhale into your entire body.... Exhale through your entire body allowing it to be heavy, heavy and limp, and just let it go..... Go deep within and find your Internal Mother. She is there. She is the great nurturer. She is the one who soothes you in times of trouble. She is the extension of your soul. She is your mother who helps you over the rough spots, who is always behind you. She is your mother consciousness. She is the mother of your being. She is that beautiful feeling of peacefulness. She is the strength and fortitude and the arms that cradle you. She is your hair. She is your skin. She is you. She is your being... your sorrow... your giving. She is your pillow and your blanket within. She is your tears... your smile. While you are here on earth, your Internal Mother is your nurturer. She smiles on you during easy times, and helps you through rough times. She is always by your side.... She is an extension of your soul. Take this time to visualize your wonderful Internal Mother. If she has a face, what would it look like?

Pause

She is the river of your energy in your body. She brings you great gifts, and with her arms extended, she caresses you from inside.... Her energy courses through your entire being from your feet to your head. She kisses you... loves you... soothes you... surrounds you in love... carries you. She is your Internal Mother of light and love. Be with her now and feel her loving presence.

Pause

Tell your Internal Mother that you have trust in her. Say, "You are mother soul. I am the child of your existence. I give myself to you to caress, to nurture, to love. You are me and I am you. We are one. I lose myself in you. It matters not, for I am you. I give myself wholly to you and ask only this: Fill me with your love as you hold me in your arms. I am you, and you are me. Together we shall build a ship of everlasting beauty and accomplishments... and go together as one across the ocean of life and travel the many miles of this glorious earth. I am the ship, you are the water. I guide the ship, and you blow the wind into my sails. I glide across the surface, but you make smooth sailing. For you are I and I am you.... We sail the seas, embracing, with arms around each other. Yours around me... mine around you. I take you with me wherever I go.... Thank you Internal Mother for your constant presence in my life."

Reflect now on your dialogue with your Internal Mother. Appreciate her vigilance and love.

Pause

As you begin to stretch and return to conscious state, know that you will always love and accept your Internal Mother, and that she is there for you whenever you need her.

18

Knowing Love

Guide: Gerald G. Jampolsky, M.D.

*"God's presence can only be
experienced in the present instant."*

Introduction

Love can only be reached in the present, and it is only through love that we can reach beyond time to timelessness....

Our ego-mind, however, uses time for a very different purpose. Its purpose is to judge, to attack, and to separate.... [But] *A Course in Miracles* suggests that the true purpose of time is to recognize that "God's will for us is perfect happiness," right now.

The Journey

I can know love only in the present. My preoccupation with the past and its projection into the future defeat my aim of present peace. Peace cannot be found in the past or future, but only now, is this instant. The past is over and the future is yet to be.

1. Write down three ways you can give your love to others today without expecting anything in return. Select one of

these ways and actually commit yourself to sharing your love with someone today.

2. For just one instant today, focus on accepting the peace of God as your only goal. Remind yourself that God is never in the past or future, but only in the present. You can accept His peace now.

3. At least twice today practice the following "messenger of truth" process.

> Imagine that the entire universe is made up only of light and that you are at the center of that light — in the heart of God. Recognize that your only reality is light. Now, while staying in the consciousness of that light, step into the world of illusion on the planet earth. Imagine that during that one second you are on earth, all you have to do is let your light shine on and through all minds. Then step back into the center of light once again. For that one, brief instant, while you were in the world of illusion, know that you were a messenger of God — a messenger of truth — bringing love and light to a world filled with fear and darkness.

Remember that as a messenger of truth you don't have to judge or evaluate, you don't have to do anything, except let the Christ-light shine through.

4. For just one moment let everything else go from your mind. Now — in this instant — accept the joy that is your natural inheritance as a bringer of light to others.

Patricia Hopkins and William N. Thetford worked with Gerald Jampolsky on the creation of Goodbye to Guilt. *Hopkins is the* co-author with Dr. Jampolsky of a series of articles, "To Give is to Receive" published recently in Unity Magazine. Thetford is responsible as coscribe with Helen Schucman, Ph.D. for A Course In Miracles. Gerald Jampolsky, M.D., best-selling author and physician, founded The Center for Attitudinal Healing in Tiburon, California.

19

Relationships

Guide: Mona O'Neal

*"We are fundamentally whole and capable of great love;
we bring that wholeness with us when
we join the dance of life."*

Introduction

The most basic need today seems to be a feeling of genuine connection with our fellow human beings. This meditation helps access the subconscious to overcome the insecurity of the conscious mind around reflection. Every person who has ever touched our lives has brought us an opportunity to learn, and we are the total of that learning and as such, are whole, perfect. We can never be without love, because we are an embodiment of love. As we give love, so then, do we receive.

Through this meditation, clients are able to put old or present relationships into perspective and deal with issues of co-dependency and control. They begin to "lighten up" and see that all of life is a dance... if we can only listen for the music.

The Journey

Find a place to sit or lie down in a comfortable position. Do not use the bed because you do not want to fall asleep. Loosen any tight clothing and begin to sink into your chair or the floor, taking several deep, relaxing breaths and letting them out naturally. It is safe here. All is well. With each exhale, feel yourself becoming more and more relaxed... more relaxed... at peace.

Imagine now that you are walking along a well-tended path through a beautiful flower garden. The bright sunshine is warm on your skin and a cool breeze is dancing through flowers of every color and description. Their aromas mix together in an intoxicating perfume. The insects work and play in harmony in this profusion, and the birds have come to feed from this bounty and to joyfully sing their grace. The petals drop silently from a deep, red rose. Catch one and bring its velvety, soft sweetness to your cheek. In this moment, you feel at one with the garden... in perfect relationship with each flower, each creature, each ray of sunlight, each breath of air touching your skin. Savor the moment and walk on along the path.

Pause

There is music playing nearby and sound of laughter. As you follow the turn of the garden path, you see that it is a large festive party on the grounds of a magnificent mansion. You are beckoned to join in the occasion. Somehow, everyone there seems strangely familiar. You find all of your close friends, your relatives, and your business associates among the group.... Everyone you have ever known is here.... Those who are living and those who have gone on have all come to this party, and you are the guest of honor. Your host explains that you are here to receive a lifetime achievement award, and each one present has had some part in helping you achieve this goal. The host asks that you choose the six most important people in your life to share the head table. Who will they be? Choose them now.

Pause

All who came are being shown inside the great banquet hall. The music is lively and happy. The hall is elegantly prepared for the banquet feast. You are seated at the head table with the six most important people in your life. There is an atmosphere of joy and anticipation as the banquet proceeds. You have time to speak to each one of these special guests and to hear their responses as the musicians play and the food is served. What are you saying to them? What do they say to you? To each other? Who did you not invite to be in this honored position? Why not? Listen to these conversations and enjoy this time of celebration now for the moment.

Pause

Now it is time for the presentation of the award. You hear the host telling the guests about all the things you have accomplished in your life. "Today we have come here to honor this very special person for the lifetime achievement of _____." As you accept the award and thank all of the people who came to honor you, look at the expressions of love and pride in their eyes. Feel the joy in your own heart for what you have accomplished and know that this honor is completely authentic and well-deserved. This is what you came into this life to do and everyone here has had some part in empowering you to reach this achievement.

As the banquet is finished, the party is gradually moved

toward the grand ballroom. The doors, marked "LIFE" in huge golden letters, swing open slightly to each one entering. Walking through the doors, something wondrous happens. The body and the outer clothing of the ego simply evaporate. What you are here is a complete and perfect circle of golden light and, at the center a dazzling jewel that gives off a warm, glowing light. The circle is you, whole, perfect and complete and the jewel at the center is love. Each circle that appears in the room has its own glowing jewel center of love. Each guest at the banquet is now transformed into a golden circle of light. These circles may be spouses, lovers, parents, children, or friends. Each one is its own complete and perfect self and each one has come here to the dance of life to bring joy, fulfillment, wisdom, and unique expression. In this moment when the goal of survival is forgotten, love is given for its own sake. As the music of life urges us onward, our dance is filled with relationships of all kinds. In each one there is the potential for great joy and great pain, and you see that only in the depth of such caring is true joy possible.

As the circles move about the floor, many never really touch, but all share in the music and the light. Some touch only briefly and move on. Some circles cover one another completely and appear to become one circle... but which one? Others cover or are covered just enough to blot out the light from both centers and soon grow cold and end their dance. Fearing such closeness but cursing the dark, they soon move on looking to find a new light, new warmth of human contact and to join again in the dance. At last each one discovers that is a whole, perfect, and complete circle with its very own special light at the center. It is now and was always vibrant, radiant, and alive... just eclipsed for a while in fear. Sometimes two perfect circles meet and know that gently touching side by side they can move together in the dance, and with their lights combined can in some extraordinary way change the world.

And the song they sing is here. "Pure love is at the center of my life. Love is what I am. Never less. Always more. Love is what I am. I cannot give to you what you do not already have. I do not ask you what I cannot give myself. Never less, always more. Love is what I am."

Each glowing circle of light in its own unique perfection now moves through the dance of life, lights honoring lights, hearts touching hearts, lightly, joyfully. "Love is what I am."

Now we must bring the dance and the dancers back into this time and place with the body wearing its ego clothes in tact. As I count to five, you will become fully awake and alert. One... breathe deeply and wiggle your toes... two... move your shoulders and arms... wiggle your fingers... three... another deep breath... move your head from side to side... four... open your eyes and look around... five... stand up and stretch.

Mona O'Neal is a Religious Science Practitioner in Vista, California. She writes and conducts workshops on meditation, visualization, self-esteem, and other personal growth issues. Her guided imageries, "Meditation in the Real World - 15 Minutes at a Time," are available on tape with musical background. An order form is in back of this book.

Healing

20

Adversity

Guide: Bernie S. Siegel, M.D.

*"An inspiring meditation that will motivate you
to take control of your life."*

Introduction

Much of your life is created by messages that you have
received at an early age. Those of us who confront adversity,
afflictions, and do not fear failure, have often been programmed by our parents and other authority figures in our
lives. I am told that the famous psychiatrist, Carl Jung, when
his friends would come to him with good news, would say,
"Perhaps if we stick together, we can get you through this."
And when they would appear and say, "Carl, I've lost my
money, I've been fired from my job," he would say, "Let's
open a bottle of wine, something good will come of this."
Why would Norman Vincent Peale write a book called *The
Power of Positive Thinking*? Why – because his mother said to
him, "Norman, if God slams one door, farther down the
corridor another is opened." We have to realize how much
our parents program us, so that for some of us there can be
no failure. Life can only offer us re-directions. My parents
would say to me, when I came home with problems, "It's
meant to be, something good will come of this. God is
redirecting you." And I would go to my room and wait for
God to show me the new direction.

Those kinds of messages allow a young man named Jason to say, "If God wanted me to be a basketball player, He would have made me seven feet tall. But He gave me cancer so I'd write a book and help other people." The Bible also tells us that adversity opens you to a new reality, and afflictions heal. The universe becomes a very different place for those who have been brought up with these kinds of messages, and if you haven't been, you can re-parent yourself. You can choose to be your own parent and give yourself a new degree, CD or CM, the chosen dad or chosen mom, and then choose to make your universe a very different place to live in.

The Journey

So create a safe, comfortable place for yourself. You don't have to move to take a trip. Let your eyes close gently, let my voice go with you through this healing interval. The time and images, visions and dreams, the language of the mind and body, the language of our creator. This is not a time for guilt or fear. You cannot do this wrong. Taking the time for yourself is an important message, and the mind and body will know that you are interested in living and healing yourself and your life. So take a moment now, and gently close your eyes if you haven't, and let my voice go with you, as you begin your journey. Let's begin by creating your universe. You're at the center of an enormous sphere with no circumference. It touches all other spheres. And see this center in the corner of the universe, in the middle of nowhere, and you will be the only person who knows where the middle of nowhere is. Take a moment here, before you begin your journey, to strengthen yourself by absorbing the energy from the earth and sky from this very special corner at the center of an enormous sphere, and allow every cell in your body to fill with love and light and energy for this journey. Just as a beehive has every cell filled with honey, fill your body, and take moment to prepare it for the journey ahead. And open every cell, and move down through your body, filling it with light and love and energy.

Pause

Notice that it's morning in this corner of the universe. The sun is rising. It's time to get dressed for a new day. We're going to school, and perhaps school fills you with fear. Another place to fail. But today we are going to a new school where there are no failures. In this school "F" stands for feedback, because you are not tested or questioned, it's simply a place to learn. And so dress for school, and as you dress be aware of what you're choosing to wear, the weave and fabric and texture, and if there are defects in the fabric of your life that may make it a difficult day, stop, and repair the defects in the fabric with love.

Pause

When you feel ready, follow my voice again, and we'll go to school. You're going to get there on your own. You can walk, use a bicycle, but under your power. And as you get closer to the school, you'll begin to meet other students who are going with you. You are not alone. We are all going to school together. Some are in a higher grade than others, but we are all learning. And as you meet the other students and move towards the classroom, don't be afraid to share with them why you are coming to school. What is it that you really need to learn about? And you'll notice as you enter the school that each room has a label on the door, of the subject that will be taught in that room. And walk through the corridors until you find the room with the subject you feel you need to learn about. Even if you're the only student in that room, the teacher will appear. Get to know the room. It's a place where many wonderful things can happen. The blackboard, the bulletin board, the desks, the windows, other students coming into the room, perhaps you know them, and the sounds from outside the classroom. This is a special school, there's no limit on the age of the students. Anyone may come to your class.

Then the door opens and a teacher appears. Who is the teacher? The teacher will pick up a piece of chalk and write on the blackboard. And what is the lesson about? What are you here to learn? And what you ultimately learn, and the teacher will help you, is that each room has its own chemistry. Each room is full of solutions, and the teacher will always be there to help you find your solutions. Every problem, every fear, has a solution. You only need to find the right one for yourself. And think of your greatest fear, your greatest problem, and walk over to the cabinet that's in the room and pick a solution for your fear or problem. And just as an acid can be neutralized with the proper solution, all of your fears and problems can be neutralized too.

And when the teacher is done discussing solutions, you'll be asked to come up to the blackboard and write down what you think your homework should be about. Make a list of all the things you need to work on at home, things that need to be resolved, removed, healed, and perhaps on another part of the blackboard write down the solutions that will apply to your homework, and take a moment for yourself to do this. Allow your feelings to help you solve the problem, to see what needs to be said and done, so that each of those can be erased from your life. And when you think of a solution, take the eraser and clean the slate, and you'll realize as you work at this, that soon the blackboard is free of problems, and then, draw a great big heart on that part of the blackboard. The bell rings to let you know the class is over, and each time you hear the bell breathe in peace and focus yourself for the next step. Gather up any papers or notes you have made, and take them with you out of this school room, onto a new path. A path where there are no failures, only attempts, only reworkings, but no failures. Where the word try appears with a capital "T", and each time you try you can only fail better, and better, and better, until there are no failures in your life.

Pause

Continue on your path and journey, taking you back towards home, and as you walk along the path, move into the right lane, make the right turns. You will always know what feels right. When you come to a fork in the road, take it, and you find coming towards you some young boys dressed in uniforms. And as they come closer you realize they are cub scouts. And I want you to ask them what their motto is, and they will tell you, "Do your best." Just as the Bible tells us, Jeremiah visited a potter, and he just worked and reworked his clay. That's all we're asking. For you to work with what you've been given, to create the best shape and the best result you're capable of. And when your path finally leads you home, go into the den, or the living room or your bedroom. You'll find an old photo album, and there will be many photographs of the past. And I want you to put some of the future in, because you know where you are headed, you are creating your future. And do not be afraid of it. You are in the game of life, sometimes the game gets a little rough, but there is no mention of failure, no fear of adversity. When you get the opportunity to play, play as well as you can, so that someday you will not be sorry you didn't give it all you had. And when you feel ready, pick a moment to find a comfortable place in the house, and just stretch out for a moment and rest, and think of the value that adversity and afflictions can play if they redirect you and push your reset button. Unfortunately, our way of changing is to respond to difficulties, but if you install a reset button in yourself, the difficulties will reset you and you will move on in a healthy direction, feeling much better. And take a moment to practice.

Pause

Think of something that you're afraid of, and then push your button and allow a feeling of peace and love and beauty and light to move through you, washing out the fear. And just as you cleaned the slate at school, cleanse yourself. That reset button works very much like an eraser. And when difficulties occur, there is no issue of guilt or blame or shame.

Pause

When a head of lettuce grows, we don't blame the lettuce if one head is larger or greener than another. There are many circumstances that go into creating a head of lettuce. Then you are free to untie the knots of fear, to break the habits, and to create some beautiful fruit in your life. So don't be afraid to fertilize yourself, to feed yourself, and to use all the things that come into your life. For you to grow and bloom and blossom and bear fruit, it's no different than a fruit tree which needs to be fertilized, which needs rain, which accepts the sunshine, and they all go together to create the perfect result. And when you can visualize that tree growing, blossoming, blooming and bearing fruit, allow it to become a part of you. Get to know how unique and beautiful you are amongst all the other trees. And if at any time in your life you feel that you are being overwhelmed with adversity or fear, within you is a soft voice coming from a wizard, a very wise soul that lives in you, who knows all and who can't fail. And so when times are difficult, remember to go inside yourself, because within you is also a classroom, and sitting there will be the wizard, and you might want to take a moment to consult the wizard now, to help guide you.

Pause

When, and only when, you are done visiting with the wizard, allow yourself to come back, allow yourself to be aware of your own breathing. Each breath will bring you more peace, more awareness, until you finally are awake, aware and alert. And return to the room by opening and becoming a new I.

Bernie S. Siegel, M.D., attended Colgate University and Cornell University Medical College. His surgical training took place at Yale New Haven Hospital and the Children's Hospital of Pitts-burgh. He has published two bestselling books, Love, Medicine, and Miracles (1986), *and* Peace, Love and Healing (1989) *In 1993, his third book,* How to Live Between Office Visits *will be published. Bernie now travels extensively with his wife, Bobbie, undertaking a heavy schedule of speaking engagements and workshops, where he shares his ideas, techniques, and experiences regarding the roles of love and understanding in self-healing.*

21

Effective Prayer

Guide: James V. Goure

"You are one with all that is."

The Introduction

"Effective Prayer" was developed as a technique for anyone to use to achieve greater good for oneself, for everyone, and for everything. The author told people, "Use this prayer fifteen minutes in the morning and fifteen in the evening for two weeks, and I guarantee you a miracle." The miracles that have resulted from the use of this prayer appear infinite in number.

The Journey

❋   I release all of my past, negatives, fears, human relation-ships, self-image, future, human desires, sex, money, judgment and communication to the Light.

❋   I am a Light Being.

❋   I radiate the Light from my Light Center throughout my being.

✸ I radiate the Light from my Light Center to everyone.

✸ I radiate the Light from my Light Center to everything.

✸ I am in a bubble of Light and only Light can come to me and only Light can be here.

✸ Thank you God for everything, for everyone and for me.

James V. Goure gave the world tremendous spiritual treasures, but lived a full life in the physical as well. He was a graduate of the U.S. Naval Academy and served as a commander in the Navy shortly after World War II. He held a number of government positions, including senior executive officer of the Atomic Energy Commission. In 1976, he and his wife, Diana, founded United Research in Black Mountain, North Carolina, to promote the use of prayer for the greater good of all. In December 1986, Goure passed away, but his legacy continues.

22

Embracing Physical Pain

Guide: Niro Markoff Asistent

"The best way to deal with physical pain is to... experience it fully and completely."

Introduction

Through her own battle with AIDS, Niro Markoff Asistent learned the lessons available from dealing directly with her physical pain. "Many of us are more afraid of physical pain than death itself. This is an area where it is important to acknowledge our limitations and recognize that the extreme approach rarely works. When we are willing to keep meeting the pain moment by moment, we can determine the appropriate use of medication. It is a process of awareness through acceptance.... The best way to deal with physical pain is to experience it fully and completely. This facilitates the movement of its energy. Unfortunately this often goes directly against our instinct to hold our breath and tense our body to keep pain at a distance...," she writes.

As you begin this meditation, "the pain may feel like a concrete block of dark energy. But when you are willing to stay with it, simply breathing into it, [you] may be surprised that this solid mass may become less dense." This meditation is a guide for exploring physical pain and how to move it from "dark to less dark."

81

The Journey

Lie down on your back on your bed and close your eyes.

The following text should be read aloud by a friend:

Please breathe deeply and bring your full attention to your breath. Let yourself feel your own presence to the best of your ability. Become aware of what is happening in and around you. The sound, the smells, the sensations.

Pause

Now open up and go beyond your five senses. Let yourself be open to your intuition and to guidance from your inner healer. As you continue to breathe deeply, begin to focus on the light within. Visualize a beautiful, shimmering white light, representing the presence of God. Trust whatever image your subconscious brings forth; this is simply a guideline. The color may be purple or blue or green, just let it be whatever it is. Let yourself be in the presence of God. Let the light bathe you.

Pause

As you begin to feel safe and your body becomes more and more relaxed, become aware of the center of the pain that is affecting you."

Take a deep breath. As you continue to breathe, let the light enter your body and comfort you. Let the comforting sensation fill all the parts of your body that are not in pain, so that the painful area becomes more and more precise. Bring your full awareness to the center of your pain. Feel the specific location of the pain and notice how it feels different from the rest of your body.

Pause

Now allow yourself to draw healing energy and strength from the parts of your body that are not in pain. Request God's guidance and support in this process.

Take a deep breath. Continue to breathe deeply as you go deeper and deeper into the pain. It might be very scary, as if the pain will be too much. Trust the guidance of God and keep on going. Now you can only feel the pain in its full intensity.

Remember to continue to breathe deeply even though your tendency will be to tense up and hold your breath. Now observe what color the pain is. Trust whatever image comes.

Pause

Now what is the dimension of it? What is its form? What is its size?

As you continue to breathe, see the pain in its full reality. Keep focusing on the form, size, and intensity of the pain. Your body may want to cry, let it cry, or scream or sigh. Simply let it happen. Let the energy move.

Now, asking for the full assistance of the light within you, using your full creative power, see the pain become smaller, the color paler, and the intensity softer.

Take a deep breath. Feel the pain now. Maybe it is throbbing.

If it is, feel the pulse. Watch its dance of contraction and expansion. The intensity followed by stillness, in and out, in and out. Feel the pain beginning to be supple. Again with the guidance of God, and at your own pace, use your creative power to visualize the pain becoming smaller.

Take a deep breath. As the pain diminishes, let yourself rest in the lesser intensity of the pain. Simply concentrate on your breath and on your body resting on your bed. Give yourself a break. Let your body take a break.

Pause

Now once again, using your creative power, visualize the light inside of you, healing the pain completely, and let yourself fall into a state of rest. Let yourself be with God. God is always ready, always there for us. We need only to get out of the way. It is our choice to remember that we can let go. We do not have to suffer. We can be open to the support of our friends and loved ones, as well as to God. Let yourself spend time in deep appreciation of yourself and of God.

Niro Markoff Asistent is a therapist in private practice in New York City. She is the Founding Director of SHARE (The Foundation for Self Healing AIDS Related Experiment), and she lectures and leads workshops all over the country.

23

Healer Within

Guide: Michael K. Wilson

"A way to awaken your own natural self-healing abilities."

Introduction

This guided meditation can produce a peaceful state of mind and expanded awareness of your inner healing potential. It can help and support efforts to achieve and maintain positive results in all areas of your life. For best results, this meditation should be used daily for ninety days in order to help shift your self-awareness and subconscious mind into a more positive expanded state of self-love and self-healing. This meditation has been used extensively by people with AIDS and other life-threatening illnesses.

The Journey

Find a location in which you are not likely to be disturbed. Choose a quiet place where you can lie down and be very comfortable and very relaxed.

Close your eyes and focus your awareness on your breathing. Make no attempt to change it or to alter it, just become aware of it. Follow the breath as it comes in your nostrils, down into your lungs, and pushes the chest out and back, out again. Notice how soothing and relaxing the breath is.

Focus your awareness on the energy that is in your breath. Once again follow this energy that is in your breath as it comes in the body, fills up the lungs, and pushes the chest out and back out again. You become aware of your own breathing process, and this places the power and the energy of your life force in your thoughts. Divine energy is in every breath you take. With each breath you now take, you begin to release all tension and all stress from your mind and from your body.

Your subconscious mind is the builder of your mental immune system and your physical body. It has the power to heal you, and your thoughts are the source behind that power.

With each breath you take you are safe, surrounded, protected, and divinely guided by infinite intelligence and infinite unconditional love from within. If you have been denying yourself self-love, self-approval, and self-acceptan e in your life whether though guilt, shame, anger, non-forgiveness of yourself or of others, you have been blocking the unlimited healing power of the healer within. We are going to move past all guilt, shame, anger, and non-forgiveness, and we are going to release all false illusions created out of fear. You are going to leave behind all restrictions and all limitations, and you are going to use the unlimited healing power of self-love as the vehicle to travel inward and awaken this great and grand healer within.

Every single facet of your physical reality and all its experiences come from one infinite single source. That source is you. It is eternal and beyond all limits in its energy to generate its own reality and experiences.

Refocus on your breathing, and this time, notice the complete and total relaxation that is beginning to flow throughout your mind and throughout your body with each breath you take. It is also time for you to understand that this is the gateway to within.

Pause

We are going to enter into a higher level of consciousness and self-awareness where you will fully understand that you are unlimited in your ability to use the power of your mind to heal your physical body and all areas of your life. This healing power has never been outside of yourself but has always been within.

You are going to move out of mass programming, mass thinking, and mass control and move into individual self-awareness, individual power, and individual freedom. The body constantly heals itself. It is a self-healing, self-regulating system, and you are the source of the power behind this system. There is no difference between the energy that shapes your ideas and your experiences or the energy that heals you when you are sick. This healing energy and power come from one unlimited infinite source, and that source has always dwelled within you.

You now call upon this source to help you in the healing process. There is no time or space to your thoughts. Your thoughts are not finite; your thoughts are infinite. We are all inter-connected with the same infinite and unlimited source that is within each one of us. We are all part of one magnificent creation. We are all of one mind and all healing is self-healing. My healing energy for you — my positive, loving, creative thoughts about you — is directed in and through the same unlimited power of which each of us is a part. Because you, too, are a part of it, it has a positive healing effect on you, whether you are aware of it or not. Thoughts do heal.

Pause

Now once again focus on your breathing. Notice the breath once again as it comes into the body, down into the lungs, and pushes out the chest. Take this relaxing energy and send it to your feet. All stress and tension now leave your feet. Acknowledge this relaxing energy that has just floated into your feet by gently wiggling your toes. Do that now. Gently wiggle your toes. Now move this relaxing energy up into your calves, knees, and thighs. All of those areas are completely free of all stress and all tension. Your legs are beginning to get very, very heavy. Now move this relaxing energy up into your genitals, buttocks, waistline, stomach, chest, and shoulders. Now all those areas are completely flooded with this relaxing energy and all stress melts away. Move this relaxing energy down your arms, forearms, wrist, hands, and fingers. Now all those areas are very, very heavy and very relaxed as this relaxing energy floods through your arms, hands, and fingers. Acknowledge this relaxing energy by gently wiggling your fingers. Do that now; gently wiggle your fingers.

Move this relaxing energy up into your throat, your neck, jaw line, mouth, and the area around your mouth. Acknowledge the relaxing energy that is flooded into those areas by gently parting your lips and allowing some air to enter. Move this relaxing energy up into your cheeks, eyes, and eye lids. The area around the eyes and your forehead. Now your entire face and all your facial features and expressions are very, very peaceful and very, very relaxed as this relaxing energy floods over your entire face. Now send this relaxing energy into your scalp; feel your scalp tingle with this relaxing energy.

Send this energy down the base of your neck. Now your entire body is totally and completely relaxed. The body is now going into a deep, deep sleep.... It becomes very heavy, very relaxed... releasing all stress and all tension... becoming more relaxed than you have ever been.

Visualize in your mind's eye that you are drifting and floating in the vast void of space. Just drifting and floating down and down and down. Let go and give into total relaxation as your drift down deeper and deeper and down and down and down. Very peaceful, very centered and balanced and very, very relaxed. Drifting down and down and down. You are ready to take your journey inward and align yourself with the infinite source within which has created all things, becoming one with this great source and power. Knowing in reality that you have always been one in the same. Drifting and floating down and down.... You are very, very relaxed.

Pause

Now we shall recite some affirmations of love, power, strength, health, wealth, and happiness to affirm and embrace your new creative thinking, your freedom and the healer within. Silently shout out these affirmations in your mind.

"I now radiate in the healing power of unconditional love for myself and for others. My heart is now open to send this love and acceptance to others. The power to heal with love is unlimited, and I now use this unlimited power to heal myself. I now move past all limited and negative thinking, and all negativity now flows through me without affecting me. I now find it easy to forgive others and to release the past. The more I send love and healing energy and thoughts to others the more I receive. I now lovingly embrace my sexuality with healing affirmation of self-worth, self-acceptance, self-approval, and self-love. I now release all shame and all guilt that I have directed toward myself or that I have allowed others to direct toward me about my sexuality. I now cherish my sexuality as a great and grand gift. I love and I approve what I am, and what I am is great beauty and great strength.

"I now know and understand that there is absolutely nothing that cannot and has not been created by thought. I know that my thoughts are the building blocks of my future. I now choose thoughts of health, wealth, and happiness.

"I now move forward in life. I lovingly leave behind the past. I release it; I let it go. It is over and I am free. I am free from disease; I am free from all restrictions and all limitations. I have total freedom now to create love, health, wealth, and happiness in all areas of my life."

As you continue to drift down deeper and deeper and down and down and down, let go, giving in and leaving it all behind.

"I now have released all anger, all resentment, all fear, all guilt and all doubt, and I now let go of those negative emotions. I

now bring forth forgiveness, kindness, happiness, health, prosperity, inner peace, and total unconditional self-love and self-acceptance in my life. I now bring to me all that I need to be, all that I am capable of being. I make the light within me shine brighter and brighter and brighter. I am grateful for my life. I love me. I love and I approve of myself always. I am strong, I am gentle, I am loving, and I am divinely protected and guided. I am at peace with the world. I am at peace with myself. I am at peace with life."

Now an affirmation that will last you for as long as you shall live. Say to yourself: "With each breath I take, I now breathe into my body and into my life, the breath of unconditional self-love, self-approval, and self-acceptance.

Now affirm this by taking a deep breath, filling the lungs and filling the body with unconditional self-love. This affirmation will be working for you when you are awake, when you are asleep, and whether or not you are even aware of it. With each breath you now take, you will affirm self-acceptance, self-love, and self-approval in all areas of your life.

You are now completely immune, spiritually, physically, mentally, emotionally, and economically to all negative people, places, ideas, beliefs or experiences that may be around you. Self-love is self-acceptance, self-love is self-approval, self-love is self-worth, self-love is unconditional love, self-love is freedom, self-love is the greatest love of all.

Your loving and healing thoughts about yourself will keep your mind, your body, and your entire immune system strong, healthy, and vibrant. It is safe for you to be who and what you are, and you are healed inside and out. All your organs and the cells of your body are bathed in the healing power of relaxation and the infinite divine intelligence of your being. You radiate at a higher level, of energy, and with this self awareness, you now send this healing energy to every part of your body and every area of your life. You now know you have the power to heal, and you call upon this great unlimited power and infinite love within to support, to help, and to assist you in your own self healing. Your body now is being restored to perfect health... perfect health. Love, peace, health, balance, and harmony flow freely with love throughout your entire body and your mind. You now radiate in the healing power of love.

You have gone into deeper and healthier levels of the mind for healing, for rejuvenation, for energy, and for self-awareness.

As you now drift into a total and complete deep sleep, you will continue to be bathed in the healing power of self-love, self-acceptance, and self-empowerment. You now dwell in the unlimited healing power of the infinite force within which has created all things. Rest in peace, balance, and harmony, and when you awaken you will awaken into joy, health, enthusiasm, wealth, and happiness with a full understanding that love has always been the great healer.

Michael K. Wilson is a writer and self-healing facilitator in Houston, Texas. His work is drawn from studies with people like Dr. Bernie Siegel, Louise L. Hay, Ann Wigmore, Shakti Gawain, Dr. Elizabeth Kubler-Ross, and others. He offers regular classes and is also available for lectures and private consultations.

24

Soldier of Light

Guide: Larry Moen

"Declare war on your headache pain."

Introduction

Pain is something shared by all. Some people appear to have a greater tolerance than others. Or do they? Perhaps we all have great tolerance but do not make use of our healing abilities. Instead we create low tolerance by stuffing emotions. We allow those unspoken energies to eat away at our being. When our bodies can take no more, our emotions erupt into what we perceive as physical pain.

Look beyond yourself to greater things. When you remove the outer being and become just light, you will see with clarity the depths of all, and you will feel the pain no more.

The Journey

Inhale and expand your chest to twice its size.... Now exhale and reduce it to half its size.... Inhale expanding your entire body.... Exhale reducing your shape to half its size.... Inhale expanding.... Exhale reducing even more.... Inhale expanding.... Exhale reducing even smaller, and allow your small body to enter your brain stem.... You notice skies of blue and rolling hills of green. You feel the energy of life in the color green. It gives you the feeling of well being and health as it radiates from your heart area, sending renewing vibration through your blood up into your brain. You see pink and muted pastel colors turning to rose,... you feel warmth and heat throughout your entire body. You are in your mind now... the rolling hills of the brain.

Now anoint your small being in white light, healing, wonderful light. Now see that light taking the form of a tiny soldier. You are now glowing and radiant in the white light that your conscious being is sending you.

Walking through the hills down the path, notice the crevices. Walk deeper and deeper through the valleys into the brain to the spot of the pain. Notice the terrain. You are ready to release the pain...

Armor your white light soldier with anger and determination to increase the energy. Walk faster and faster, almost to the charge pace, towards the pain. You are prepared to release the pain. You are climbing and pushing, getting stronger and stronger, and pushing onward and upward.

You are at the clearing and you see the pain. You declare war against the pain. Raise your palm and illuminate the entire battlefield with white light. You stand facing the pain with your head held high watching the white light spreading well beyond the battleground.

Now let that light penetrate the pain and say to yourself, "No more pain. I am stronger than you. I am you, and I wish you to cease the pain." With that wish of determination the pain freezes and is cracked and broken into many pieces.... You gather these frozen pieces with your hands. You are master over your own pain. You hold the pieces over your head and bending back your arm, you fling outside of you where they are transformed into pure, clean energy. Now seat your soldier on a boulder where he will be posted forever, meditating on inner light always available to serve you.

Your soldier of white light is purity and goodness and love, and represents all good things. If the pain begins, ask your soldier to fight it by repeating the process. Send an energy bolt of white light into the pain, encompassing it and freezing it. Then see it crack and fall into many pieces. Gather it again and return it to the outside atmosphere where the air will obliterate it once again.

Leave your white light soldier there to do battle with the pain if it should return. For your white light soldier is stronger than the pain and will overcome it in battle every time until that pain finally gives up and loses the war.

If the pain decides to come back in another area, leave your soldier of light in the area where he or she has won, for that is his post the rest of your life. Begin a new journey starting back at the brain stem. Dispatch another soldier of light to the new area to overcome and master the new pain. You can always summon as many soldiers as you need to completely win the war on pain.

Knowing the soldiers are ready to protect you day or night, you can now leave your brain stem and return to your body. As you are again aware of your breathing, let your body expand with each breath. Growing larger and larger until you are again fully aware of yourself sitting or lying down. Stretch and enjoy how comfortable your body emotes.

25

Increase Red Cell Count

Guide: Jule Scotti Post, M.S.

"Call upon the powers of your deeper mind to create images of red blood cells being produced in your bone marrow."

Introduction

I have used this imagery to help in cancer treatment after chemotherapy. It can be used anytime a person's red blood cell count is low resulting in deep feelings of weariness and low energy levels.

The Journey

As you begin to relax, be aware of your breath flowing in and flowing out. Your chest is rising and falling. The air flows in and out of your nasal passages. Now notice the difference you feel in your muscles when you are breathing in and when you are breathing out. Notice the muscles in your legs and feet and feel the difference in these muscles as you breathe in and as you breathe out. Notice the muscles in your stomach, your chest, and your back. Feel the difference in these muscles as you breathe in and as you breathe out. Notice the muscles in your arms and hands, your neck, your head, and your face. Feel the difference in the muscles in these areas as you breathe in and as you breathe out. Each time you breathe

out, let yourself sink down deeper and deeper into relaxation... deeper and deeper into that quiet peaceful place
inside yourself where your body and mind work together in
balance and harmony. The deeper part of your mind is ready
to help you in your healing process. The deeper part of your
mind has resources and powers that can be channeled to any
part of your body and can create change and healthy growth,
renewing the life force in each cell.

In your mind's eye now call upon the powers of your deeper
mind to create images of red blood cells being produced in
your bone marrow. You may like to picture the red cells as
energetic red nurses, with crisp clean white uniforms flowing
out of your bone marrow and traveling to each cell in your
body. See these red nurses massaging each cell with strong
loving hands that soothe and comfort, restoring balance and
energy. The nurses each have a cart full of medicines and
nutrients. They have homeopathic remedies, herbal slaves,
vitamins, and medicines. Whatever you need is there. Picture these nurses feeding and nourishing each cell they have
massaged. In your mind's eye see red nurses flowing out of
the bone marrow in the long bones in your legs. A steady
stream of red nurses flows down to your feet and toes, and
they treat every cell... not one is left out. Each cell in
massaged, nourished, nurtured, and the life force within is
renewed and vibrant. Now more and more red nurses are
flowing from the bone marrow into your ankles, your calves
your knees, and your thighs. Again every cell is taken care of
in the muscles, the bone, the tissue, and the skin. The nurses
are very thorough, and they do their healing work with love
and care.

Now see the constant flow of red nurses filling your stomach,
your chest, and your back, flowing up your spinal cord and

through your nervous system. Wherever they go they massage each cell and give out whatever medicine, remedy or nutrients are needed. See them massaging and nurturing, the cells in your reproductive organs, in your large and small intestines, in your liver, kidneys, spleen, and stomach. See them massaging and nurturing each cell in your heart and lungs. Notice how these healing red nurses flow from the bone marrow in the long bones in your arms. They nurture the cells in your chest, your breasts, your shoulders, arms, and hands. Every cell is taken care of, completely massaged and nourished. Now more and more red nurses, their aprons still crisp and white, are traveling up to your neck, your head, and your face. They massage each cell and fill them with nutrients, renewing the life force within the cell walls. Your brain cells are flooded with healing red nurses, massaging, renewing, and stimulating each cell to health.

Each cell in your eyes and ears, your nose, mouth, and throat is being lovingly massaged and nourished. Not a single cell is left out. Every one of them is taken care of, and now the life force is vibrant and in full force in every cell of your body. If there is any area in your body that needs additional time, attention, loving care and healing take a few moments and call up more nurses from your bone marrow and bring them to this area. These are the most potent, competent, and caring nurses of all. They bring years of skill and wisdom and a deep love to this area of your body. As you invite them into this area let each cell open to their caring touch as the nurses massage them and feed them with nutrients. See health returning to this area as each cell becomes restored. Take as much time as you need to heal and renew this part of your body.

Pause

Now as you begin to return from this inner journey, vibrant with renewed life, these red nurses continue to flow around your body taking care of each cell even when you are not thinking about them. Whether you are awake or asleep, day or night, they will massage and nurture your body, taking special care of any area that needs to be restored to health. They will continue to nurture the life force within each cell and stimulate the flow of life energy around your body.

Now be aware again of your breathing. Notice how your body feels as you are lying down or sitting comfortably. Each time you breathe in, become more aware of the room around you and the sounds you can hear. When you are ready, open your eyes, stretch and notice how good your body feels. Go into your day or to your night's rest knowing your body is constantly being renewed and nourished.

Jule Scotti Post, M.S. is a psychotherapist who uses biofeedback and deep relaxation in the treatment of stress and chronic pain in a medical clinic in Maryland. She has a Masters in Counseling Psychology and has trained intensively in the use of guided imagery and music in therapy. She has worked in private practice as a psychotherapist for nine years and has practiced meditation for over twenty years. She has studied the principles of Chinese medicine and brings this perspective to her treatment of pain. She has recently begun training in hypnotherapy for the relief of emotional and physical pain.

26

Opening the Heart

Guide: Robert Gass, Ph.D.

"This is a guided meditation to the opening of the heart."

Introduction

This guided meditation is a simple but powerful process in which you are guided into a deeper awareness of your own heart. By using breathing techniques and visualizations of light and by calling on a higher power, energy in the heart is increased. This increased energy typically surfaces contractions or armoring around the heart.

In re-opening our hearts, we may sometimes (though not always) have the experience of releasing held-in emotion. This emotional release, when it happens, may be powerful and overt, or internal, and subtle. Emotional release is a natural part of the healing process and should be welcomed.

This guided meditation also draws upon the healing presence of those in our lives who have loved us.

The Journey

Place your body in a comfortable position. Close your eyes. Take a deep breath and hold it in.... Hold it... hold it... and let it go. Begin letting your body relax... letting your body relax. Deep breath in... hold it... hold it... and let it go, feeling your body relaxing, letting go. Once again, deep breath in... hold it... hold it... hold it... and let it go.

As you breathe in now, imagine that you can breathe directly into the center of your heart, into the area in the center of your chest that is known as the heart center. Breathe in and feel your breath come directly into this heart center. What's the first thing that you are aware of as the breath comes into the heart...? What do you feel...? What do you notice as the breath comes into the heart? As you breath, become more and more aware of your heart.

Pause

As you breathe in, imagine that you are breathing in a light of golden color. With each in-breath, experience golden light coming into your chest. Follow this golden light in with each breath and feel it come all the way into your heart center. Feel your chest beginning to fill with golden light... with each breath... golden light. This light is warm, so as you breathe in there is a sense of warmth filling your chest. With each in-breath experience warmth coming in with the breath filling your chest and heart with warmth. Very gently, with each in-breath experience this golden light and warmth filling your chest.

This golden light has healing properties to it. This light has healing properties, so as the golden light comes into your chest there is a sense of a healing touch upon your heart. With each in-breath feel this healing warm light enter your chest and gently touch your heart. It's as if you were in the hands of a master masseur or masseuse, and he or she knows your heart perfectly. Sense this golden healing light gently massaging your heart. This light is familiar. You know this light, this feeling, this healing touch. In some way, you know this... breathing in warm, golden healing light. As you become more aware of your heart, you may also become aware of places in your heart that are protected, closed, or wounded.

Breathing in golden light, you are becoming aware of places in the heart that are closed. We all have places of armoring in and around the heart, places that seem to shy away from the light as it enters. Be aware of any of these places that seem tight and be aware if there are none.

As infants, we came into this life totally open, totally vulnerable, totally alive. We met each moment without expectation and with total trust. See an image of yourself as a newborn, your eyes and your heart wide open. In your imagination remember this state of trust. See it. Feel it. Remember. Continue breathing.

But over time these innocent trusting hearts of our infant selves had experiences that taught us to fear, to close down. Remember some of these experiences that taught your heart to protect itself, that made you in some way feel like the world was not safe for an open heart.

Pause

Breathe into your heart. Breathe in warmth; breathe in light. As you breathe in, be aware of some of this armoring, for the heart carries with it the memories of the wounds of a lifetime, and in the heart there is no past and no present. In the heart it all happens now.

Breathe into your heart. Let the light illumine these places of darkness, of tightness, of numbness. Keep breathing... gently. Don't try to change what you see or experience. Keep drawing the light into your chest with each in-breath. Let your own heart now reveal to you some place in your heart where healing is needed, for which healing is available today. Let your own heart show you this place and know you are available for healing in your heart. Trust the wisdom of your own heart. Let your own heart show you this place. And now as you breathe in, breathe right into this place in your heart. Draw the light very gently up close to this place above the wounding. This healing light cannot come into your heart unwelcome. So if you wish an opening for your heart, if you wish a healing for your heart, ask in some way for this.

I invite you now to sound a prayer in your own heart, to literally say the words that ask for healing. Sound these words again and again in your heart now.

Speak them in your heart. Literally sound the words in your heart center. Ask that your heart be open, ask that your heart be healed. Call out that the spirit of all life may touch your heart. Do this in your own way again and again. It is the fervency of this call to life that will bring healing to your heart and bring love into your life. Ask again and again. You may want to put the words softly onto your lips, and as you hear the song let the words and the music come in and touch you wherever healing is needed today.

Pause

Breathe into your heart. Breathe in golden light into your heart. Be aware of any ways in which your heart has given up, any ways in which your heart has shut down or closed own in order to protect itself in opening your heart to love, you must open your heart up to all of life, and in doing so you must be willing to take risks. Sometimes you may experience pain and disappointment.

Pause

Close your eyes and in your mind's eye, see an image... the face of a person who in this lifetime — past or present — has been your great teacher of the heart... the person living or dead from whom you have most been able to receive love. See his or her face now sitting just a few feet in front of you. In your mind's eye, look up and you see his eyes looking into your eyes and remember what it feels like to be seen by these eyes that loved you in this way. As you breathe in, feel his presence right here with you in the room and remember what it feels like to be in the presence of this person who loved you in this way.

Now begin speaking to him. Speak out from your heart; holding nothing back. Tell him what is in your heart at this very moment; feel his presence here with you and let the words flow out of your heart like a river. Speak to him and say whatever is true and present in your heart at this moment. As you listen now, you can hear his voice. Remember the sound of his voice. He is speaking to you. He has come today to bring an important message... a message that your heart needs to hear. Listen and receive the message and take this message right into your heart.

Now you see that this face is being joined by other faces, one by one, all the faces of all the people of this lifetime, past and present, living and dead, who have loved you, who have been a part of the fabric of your heart and your life. They are all joining you now. You see their faces begin to appear one by one. See them.

They are all coming in response to your request, to your prayer for healing. Some of these faces will have things to say to you when they appear. You will receive these messages and bring them into your heart, and there will be some to whom you will wish to say things from your heart. You speak these words to their faces as they appear. They are all here, the faces you would expect... and possibly some that would surprise you by appearing today.

Pause

And now these beings gather in a circle around you. They form a circle of love, a circle of healing, and some them reach down their invisible hand to touch you and you feel surrounded and held by their love.

And now, one or more of these beings begin cradling you, cradling you and rocking you. Imagine yourself being held, being cradled and rocked, and being rocked and cradled and welcomed.

Breathing.... Let go of the experience of being rocked and being cradled, of being held, of being nurtured, of being welcomed.

Breath... letting go... receiving.

In your mind's eye see an image of your own heart at this moment. Feel your heart. Breathe into your heart. Breathe light into your heart. Let your own heart speak to you now. Receive the wisdom of your own heart. It may be in words.

It may be a feeling. Open and receive the wisdom of your heart. Breath... feeling your heart... feeling your heart... feeling the fullness of your being.

The guided meditation is now complete. Peace be with you.

In 1976, Dr. Gass, psychologist, teacher, healer and musician, created the Opening the Heart workshops. Since that time, more than 100,000 people have experienced his healing blend of psychology, spirituality, and music.

27

Rainbow

Guide: Karen M. Thomson, Ph.D.

"The use of color imagery enhances meditation and healing."

Introduction

The meditation, "Rainbow," has numerous healing capabilities. Healing with color and with light is very subtle, yet very powerful. This particular session affects the body's chakra system, the energy centers of the body that correspond in medical terms to the endocrine system. Red corresponds to the energy center at the base of the spine, orange to the area right below the navel, yellow to the solar plexus region, green to the heart area, blue to the throat, indigo to the midpoint of the brow, and violet to the top of the head. White Light is the protective, healing light that is the perfect blend of all colors. Focusing on these respective energy centers of the body as you visualize your journey through the rainbow can heighten the beneficial effects of this guided imagery.

The Journey

In a comfortable meditation position, take several minutes to breathe slowly and deeply, with your eyes closed, and with all concentration on your breathing. As you inhale, imagine that you are filling your body with oxygen, light, energy, and all that is positive. As you exhale, breathe out just as slowly and completely, and feel yourself letting go of the body's toxins and all negativity. Just relax and let go, and breathe very slowly and very deeply and completely.

Be aware of the deep feeling of relaxation that begins to permeate you. You may feel that your body is becoming very heavy, so heavy that it is slowly sinking into the floor.

In just a few minutes, that feeling is replaced by the feeling that you are now so light that your body begins to float up, slowly, effortlessly, higher and higher. See yourself move up through the clouds and watch the earth become smaller and smaller. You find yourself far out in the cosmos, suspended, continuing to float in space. You are aware of no physical sensations except a feeling of freedom, of weightlessness. You feel no fear. You feel absolute trust and protection, for you have the inner knowing that you are filled and surrounded by Light and Love. You hear yourself saying,

> The Light of God surrounds me;
> The Power of God protects me;
> The Peace of God enfolds me;
> The Love of God empowers me.
> The Presence of God is with me always.
> Where I am, God is. All is well.

Imagine, see with the mind's eye, feel with your inner knowingness that you are far out in space, far from Earth. You look back at Earth, and it appears as a small ball of beautiful blue-green light about the size of your fist. Now see the Earth as surrounded in a rose-pink Light. This is a Light of Protection, of Love, and of Peace, in essence a prayer for the planet without words that uses Light. You are gently, peacefully continuing to float in an indigo, a dark blue-purple outer space, punctuated by particles of light in the far off distance. Some of these lights are stars and planets. You even see a moving galaxy composed of a myriad lights, a breath-taking and awesome sight. You are enjoying the splendor of your view, and simultaneously very peaceful feelings of your expansive experience in space. All of a sudden you feel as if you are being pulled back to Earth, gently yet powerfully, as if you were a magnet and Earth were a larger magnet that is undeniably attracting, calling you back to Earth. Knowing that you are being drawn back to Earth signifies that your mission, your divine and unique purpose for being on the Earth at this time is not yet complete. You accept the "pull" and enjoy the "ride" of returning to the Earth's atmosphere.

As you begin your slow descent through the first couple layers of clouds and into the warm sunlight, you find yourself in a brilliant, soft blue sky dotted with large puffs of clouds. All of a sudden, your attention is captivated by the biggest and most beautiful rainbow you have ever seen. Feeling some ability to steer your course, you head toward the rainbow and its beautiful colors. You find yourself slowing, gliding into the first color of the rainbow, which is red. You pause in the midst of the rainbow, totally immersed and surrounded in the color red. You breathe in the color red and take in all the positive aspects of the color red. Feel yourself, see or imagine yourself filled and surrounded by the color red. Be the color red.

When you have derived all the positive attributes of red, feel yourself floating out of red and into the next color, which is orange. Again, feel yourself pausing in the color orange. All you can see is orange. Breathe in orange; imagine being filled and surrounded with orange, and be the color orange, a beautiful shade of orange.

When you have taken in all of the positive attributes of orange, find yourself moving into the next color, which is yellow, a beautiful shade of yellow. Here, totally surrounded by yellow, you take a deep breath of pure yellow light. See yourself as being filled and surrounded by yellow light.

When you have absorbed all of the healing, positive energies of the color yellow, feel yourself gliding on to the next color, green. In the middle of the rainbow, take a deep breath and totally fill yourself with the wonderful healing energies of green, the color of growth, creativity.

After you have basked in the green light and bathed in its essence, feel yourself gently floating into the next color, which is a beautiful sky blue. Move until you are totally immersed in the blue light. Breathe it in and see it completely surrounding your body. Be the blue healing light.

When you have derived all of the benefits from blue, continue moving, gliding into the next color, which is indigo, dark bluish-purple. See, feel only this color, this light filling and surrounding your body.

When you have been permeated with this color and received all of its benefits, move into the next color which is violet. Linger in this color a short time, breathing it in, filling and surrounding the body. Then move into the last color — a blend of all colors: a most beautiful, radiant white Light. Here you stay — rested, rejuvenated, relaxed, yet invigorated — as long as you like.

Pause

When it is time to leave, you take a deep breath and feel yourself back in the place where you began your meditation. Again, you breathe, and this time give your body a good stretch and open your eyes. Remember the healing you have just had with the Light and with color. With gratitude and feeling GREAT, you prepare to go about the rest of your day.

From the early '70s through the early '90s, Karen Thomson has blended an academic career with her metaphysical work. As a full professor with her Ph.D. in English, she taught literature and composition in the college classroom and was also a college administrator in the university system of Georgia. In 1993, she made a dramatic shift in her career and became a full-time practitioner of various metaphysical and healing arts including psychic readings, spiritual counseling, and healing. She lectures, teaches, writes, and provides private counseling.

28

Ring of Light

Guide: Ernestine Wolfe-Cline

"The Ring of Light cleanses and clears."

Introduction

The Ring of Light guided journey is used to clear and purify the auric field and to align all bodies and chakras. It balances and heals the whole energy field.

The Journey

Sit quietly with your back straight, feet flat on the floor, and hands in your lap, palms up.

Focus your attention on your breath and breathe slowly and deeply, but gently. Be gentle with yourself.

Allow your breath to become pure radiant light. Draw it into every cell of your body. See your physical form filled with brilliant light. Continue the breathing and allow each breath to expand the light beyond the physical form until you are surrounded in a white radiance. See your sphere of energy as a great ball of light. Know that this is your true essence.

Pause

Maintain your sphere of light. Bring your attention into the center of your sphere and move into the sacred sanctuary of your inner temple. Know that this is the dwelling place of the Spirit of God.

Pause

Bring your attention into the center of your sphere of energy. Find yourself in a beautiful place called "Peace." Feel the sacred energy of this place.

In this beautiful place, you become aware of a radiant beam of light that pours down upon you from an infinite point in the universe. The stream of light washes over you and fills you. It forms a ring or circle of light, a white flame about three inches high and four feet in diameter that encircles your feet. This ring of fire hums as it vibrates and begins to ascend and surround your body with a soft warm glow. The Ring of Light moves up to the level of the hips and hesitates. A sphere of blue light is placed at the energy center at the base of the spine. It's cool, calm, blue energy radiates through your body.

Pause

The Ring of Light moves upward and hesitates once again at the level of the navel. This energy center is filled with a sphere of golden orange light, and it vibrates throughout your body with a gentle nurturing energy.

Pause

The Ring of Light begins to ascend once again and moves to the level of the solar plexus and stands at this level. The solar plexus center is filled with a lovely, rich, green light. Allow it to flow through this energy center. Now in the center of that energy point is placed a radiant, gleaming emerald. Feel its jewel-toned energy move through you.

Pause

The outer Ring of Light then moves upward to the level of the heart center. In the heart center is placed a sphere of deep, rosy, pink light. That sphere expands to fill the chest cavity with that rosy glow. In the center of the heart energy point is placed a beautiful white rose.

Pause

The outer Ring of Light once again moves upward until it comes to the level of the neck and throat and here, it hesitates once more. The neck is surrounded by a band of blue light. The blue light moves into the neck and throat and collar bone area. Feel the blue light move through the neck, throat, collar bone, tongue, jaws, and teeth. At the center of this energy point — the center of the collar bone and neck — is placed a magnificent golden butterfly.

Pause

The outer ring of fire ascends again to move to the level of the forehead and hesitates here. In the center of the forehead is placed a clear white crystal; its vibration moves through the forehead and eyes as a pale blue-white light.

Pause

The Ring of Light moves upward once again to the level of the top of the head, circling the crown. In the top of the head is placed a sphere of white light. As you observe it more closely, you see many diamond points of light within the sphere.

Pause

The outer Ring of Light ascends higher and draws unto itself just above the head to form another white sphere about six inches above your head. It begins to pour forth beams of liquid light that flow around you as a great fountain.

This liquid light forms a great shield around you. In silence, experience your own fountain of light.

Pause

Begin to focus your attention on your breath. Allow the image of the fountain to begin to fade. Become more aware of your breath. Allow your breath to attune to the hum of the universe as you draw your attention back to the physical world around you. Take as much time as you need to gently and fully bring back your awareness. Move gently and easily only when you are ready.

Ernestine Wolfe-Cline, who resides in Fort Myers, Florida, is a minister, artist, and teacher who uses her intuitive and artistic abilities to assist others in their search for greater awareness and spiritual direction in their lives. She has developed a meditative process for creating artworks and teaching others to express their own creativity through drawing and painting. Her artworks are found in most of the fifty United States and eleven foreign countries.

Relaxation & Stress Release

29

Conditioned Relaxation

Guide: David E. Bresler, Ph.D.

"Breathing is literally the way of life."

Introduction

Each time we breathe, we draw oxygen into the body's cells and tissues, where it is used in the burning of the body's fuel and the production of energy.

Proper breathing can actually help to control negative emotions, including anger, hatred, jealousy, grief, and frustration. Simply by slowing down the rhythm of breathing, which in turn reduces the heart rate, you can often eliminate tension, nervousness, and pain altogether.

Keep in mind that there are two ways to breathe – from your chest and from your abdomen. For this exercise, try to breathe only from your abdomen, meaning that your stomach will move in and out with each breath you take. Allow your breathing to become slow and rhythmic.

The Journey

Before beginning, take a moment to get comfortable and relax.... Sit upright in a comfortable chair and loosen any tight clothing or jewelry or shoes that might distract you. Make sure you won't be interrupted for a few minutes.... Take the telephone off the hook if necessary.... Now take a few slow, deep abdominal breaths... inhale... exhale... inhale... exhale....

Focus your attention on your breathing throughout this exercise, and recognize how easily slow, deep breathing alone can help to produce relaxation. Let your body breathe itself, according to its own natural rhythm.... Slowly and deeply....

Now let's begin the exercise with what we call a "signal breath," a special message that tells the body we are ready to enter a state of deep relaxation. The signal breath is taken as follows.... Exhale... take a deep breath in through your nose... then blow it out through your mouth.

You may notice a kind of "tingling" sensation when you take the signal breath. Whatever you feel is a signal or message to your body that will become associated with relaxation, so that as you practice this exercise over and over again, simply taking the signal breath alone will produce the same degree of relaxation that you'll be able to get by completing the entire exercise.

Breathe slowly and deeply... as you concentrate your attention on your breathing, focus your eyes on an imaginary spot in the center of your forehead... look at the spot as if you are trying to see it from the inside of your head.... Raise your eyes way up so as to stare at that spot from the inside of your head. Concentrate your attention on it.... The more you are able to concentrate on the spot, the better your relaxation response will be....

As you continue to focus your attention on the spot, you might notice that your eyelids have become quite tense.... That's fine, for what we want to do is to teach your body the difference between tension and relaxation. Your eyelids are controlled by some of the smallest muscles in your body, and they become easily tired and fatigued as they become more and more tense. When I count to three, we'll demonstrate the difference between tension and relaxation by allowing your eyelids to close gently, allowing the feelings of tension to melt away quickly.

One... two... three... close your eyelids firmly but not too tightly, and as they close, sense a soothing feeling of relaxation radiate all around your eyes... the top of your eyes... the bottom... the sides... the front and back....

Breathe slowly and deeply.... Feel the relaxation in your eyes, and how nice it feels.... Let these feelings of gentle relaxation radiate all around your eyes and out to your forehead... to your scalp... all around the back of your head... to your ears and temples... to your cheeks and nose... to your mouth and chin... and around to your jaw.... As you feel all the tension flow out of your face and the area around your mouth, relax your jaw muscles.... As you do so, let your jaw gently open slightly so that all the tension can smoothly flow away....

Remember your breathing, slowly and deeply.... Relax the muscles in your neck, and as you relax the back of your neck, let your head tip gently forward until your chin just about touches your chest.... As you do so, feel all the tension flow away from the muscles in the back of your neck.... Let this nice, gentle feeling of relaxation now radiate down into your shoulders.... Feel the heaviness of your shoulders on your trunk as the shoulder muscles gently relax.... This is one of the most important areas of the body to relax since we all tend to store a lot of tension in our necks and shoulders.... Feel all the tension flow away, and sense the nice, gentle feeling of deep relaxation....

Remember your breathing, slowly and deeply.... Let this feeling of relaxation now radiate down your arms... to your elbows... forearms... wrists... and hands.... Spend a moment to relax each of your fingers... your thumb, index finger, middle finger, middle finger, ring finger, little finger.... As your hands and arms completely and gently relax, you may notice feeling of warmth and heaviness.... Some people report pulsations or tingly sensations.... Some can even sense their heartbeat in their fingertips... others report even magnetic or pulling sensations.... Whatever you experience is your own body's way of expressing relaxation.... Remember, you cannot *force* yourself to relax, you can only *allow* yourself to relax... Trust your body... it knows what to do....

Remember your breathing. Slowly and deeply... relax your chest... and abdomen... and let this feeling of relaxation radiate around your sides and ribs, as waves of relaxation cross your shoulder blades to meet at your upper back... middle back... and lower back.... Feel all the muscles on either side of your spine softly relax.... Let your spine carry the weight of your trunk as your back muscles relax more and more deeply.... Let this feeling of gentle relaxation now radiate down into your pelvic area... to your buttocks... sphincter muscle... genitals.... Feel your whole pelvic area open up and gently relax.... Relax your thighs... knees... calves... ankles... and feet.... Spend a moment to relax each toe... your big toe, second toe, third toe, fourth toe, and little toe.... Breathe slowly and deeply.... Relax and enjoy it....

Now that your body is gently relaxed and quiet, take a moment, starting from the top of your head working down, to check lightly to see how much relaxation you have obtained....

If there is any part of your body that is not yet fully relaxed and comfortable, simply inhale a deep breath and send it into that area, bringing soothing, relaxing, nourishing, healing oxygen into every cell of that area, comforting and relaxing it.... As you exhale, imagine blowing out, right through your skin, any tension, tightness, pain, or discomfort in that area. Again, as you inhale, bring relaxing, healing oxygen into every cell of that area, and as you exhale, blow away, right through the skin, any tension or discomfort.

In this way you can send your breath to relax any part of your body that is not yet fully relaxed and comfortable as it can be.... Breathe slowly and deeply, and with each breath, allow yourself to become twice as relaxed as you were before... inhale... exhale... twice as relaxed... inhale... exhale... twice as relaxed....

When you find yourself quiet and fully relaxed, take a moment to enjoy it.... Sense the gentle warmth and feeling of well-being all through your body.... If any extraneous thoughts try to interfere, simply allow them to pass through and out of you.... Ignore them and go back to your breathing, slowly and deeply... slowly and deeply... enjoy this nice state of gentle relaxation....

Now, as you concentrate on your breathing, paint a picture in your head of how you want to be.... See yourself or any part of your body as you want it to be... freely use your imagination... see the possibilities of being exactly as you want to be... see more clearly the vision in the center of your mind's eye....

Breathe slowly and deeply.... Remember your wish, what you want for your life.... Strengthen it.... Tell yourself that "every day, in every way, I will feel better and better"....Every day, in every way, I will feel better and better.... Every day, in every way, my wish will grow stronger and stronger.... Every day, in every way, my wish will grow stronger and stronger".... Add any other suggestions you want to make yourself....

Remember your breathing, slowly and deeply.... When you end this exercise, you may be surprised to notice that you feel not only relaxed and comfortable, but energized with such a powerful sense of well-being that you will easily be able to meet any demands that arise.... To end the exercise, tell yourself that you can reach this gentle state of Conditioned Relaxation any time you wish by simply taking the signal breath... reinforce that signal breath by concluding the exercise with it... exhale... inhale deeply through your nose... blow out through the mouth... and be well.

David E. Bresler, Ph.D., former Director of the UCLA Pain Control Unit and former professor in the UCLA Medical and Dental Schools and the UCLA Psychology Department, is currently in private practice in Santa Monica, California. He is the executive director of the Bresler Center Medical Group, and Director of Research of New Health Technologies, Inc., a health research and development company.

Reprinted by permission of David E. Bresler, Ph.D. from Free Yourself From Pain, *P.O. Box 967, Pacific Palisades, CA 90272.*

30

Deep Muscle Relaxation

Guides: Edward A. Charlesworth, Ph.D.
and Ronald G. Nathan, Ph.D.

*"Deep muscle relaxation directs suggestions of relaxation
to each muscle group in turn."*

Introduction

The authors of this visualization suggest practicing a progressive relaxation exercise before beginning this deep muscle relaxation, but they indicate it is helpful not mandatory. Progressive relaxation uses muscle tensing to relax muscles, but deep relaxation relies on the power of your mind.

Drs. Charlesworth and Nathan suggest using this relaxation technique everyday. After a few sessions, you will be able to "relax needed muscles differentially while you perform tasks with needed muscles. You do not need a tight jaw or clenched fist while writing a memo at your desk."

Preparation

Spend a little time getting as comfortable as you can. While you are finding a good position, loosen any tight clothing. Loosen your shirt or blouse at the neck. Loosen your belt. If your shoes feel a little tight, take them off. Allow your eyes to close.

Mentally, you should begin to clear your mind of the business and rushing that may characterize your life. Allow a passive attitude to develop. Try to let the relaxation begin.

Open your mouth for a moment and move your jaw slowly and easily from side to side.... Now, let your mouth close, keeping your teeth slightly apart. As you do, take a deep breath... and slowly let the air slip out.

Breathing

Take another deep breath.... As you breathe out, silently say, "Relax and let go." Feel yourself floating down. Now that you are comfortable, let yourself relax even further. The more you can let go, the better it will be. Again, take a deep breath.

Pause

As you breathe out, silently say "Relax and let go." Let the air slip out easily and automatically. Already you may be feeling a little calmer. Now, just carry on breathing normally. Study your body and the feelings you are experiencing.

Pause

As you relax more and more, your breathing becomes slower. You may notice that it is slower now and that you breathe more and more from the bottom of your lungs.

It's too much trouble to move, just too much trouble to move. All tension is leaving you, and you are very comfortable. Notice that you have a feeling of well-being, as though your troubles have been set aside and nothing seems to matter.

Body Scanning

Now, as we continue, let's use the natural abilities of your mind and body to experience feelings of deep, deep relaxation. We will do this by going through your body from head to foot and progressively instilling those good feelings of relaxation. Each time you breathe out, you should feel more relaxed.

Keep your eyes gently closed. Relax your jaw muscles. Keep your teeth slightly apart and your face, neck, and shoulders loose and relaxed.

As you think about each part of your body and you allow that part of your body to relax, you will feel all the tension flowing away, and that part of your body will be comfortable, calm, and peaceful. Each time you breathe out, you will become more relaxed and feel the relaxation spreading slowly through your body.

Head and Neck Scanning

Now, think about the top of your head. Feel the area. As you breathe out, feel the top of your head relax more and more, as it becomes loose and free of wrinkles. Let tensions flow from the top of your head. The top of your head is becoming completely relaxed.

Think of your forehead. Feel the skin that covers it. Feel your eyes and the muscles that are around them. Feel those muscles relaxing more and more with each breath. Feel your forehead relaxing more and more.

Your eyelids grow heavier and quieter with each breath. Let

yourself go as you breathe gently in and out. Let the relaxation spread naturally as the tension flows out each time you exhale. Your forehead, your eyes, and all these muscles are relaxing more and more.

Feel your throat and neck. Feel them relax. As you breathe out, say, "Relax and let go." Your throat and neck are loose, quiet, and comfortable.

Shoulders and Arms Scanning

Feel your shoulders and upper back. Be aware of the skin and muscles of your shoulders and upper back. Effortlessly, allow relaxation to spread into your shoulders and upper back. With each breath you take, each time you breathe out you become more and more relaxed. The muscles are loose and comfortable. Feel quiet in your shoulder muscles.

Feel your upper arms relaxing. Feel your arms and hands. Your arms, hands, and fingers are feeling very, very relaxed. You may feel warmth or tingling in your arms and hands. Feel your arms, hands, and fingers relaxing. Feel the tension dropping from your arms, hands, and fingers.

Chest and Stomach Scanning

Now, think about your chest. Feel it. Sense the muscles under the skin around the chest. Be deeply aware of your chest. Feel relaxation spreading throughout your chest and stomach area. As you breathe out, feel the calm and relaxation in your chest. As you breathe naturally, feel relaxation and quiet in your chest and in your stomach area. Tension flows from your chest as you breathe out.

You are breathing in and breathing out. More and more you feel calm. Feel your stomach. Be aware of the skin and muscles in this area. Feel these muscles relax. Feel the tension being replaced by pleasant relaxation. As you breathe out, feel relaxation spread to your stomach and lower back.

Hips and Legs Scanning

Now feel your legs, your hips, your calves, and your ankles. Be aware of these parts of your body. Feel the muscles in these areas. Allow them to relax more and more. Let calm flow down to your legs. Feel the tension leaving. Your hips, thighs, calves and ankles are becoming loose and relaxed.

Feel your feet and your toes. Become deeply aware of your feet and of each toe. Feel how still and relaxed they are. Let all the tension leave you feet and toes.

Body Review Scanning

How does your body feel? Is it tingly? Is it heavy? Does it feel hollow? Does it feel light as if you were floating? How does your body feel?

Become aware of the tiniest feelings and try to describe these feelings to yourself. Now, for about thirty seconds or so, scan around your body for any signs of tension. If you find any tension in any muscle group, let it slip out. Try to let the tension flow and the relaxation flow in to take its place.

Pause

Think about the ocean as you continue to scan your body for tension. Imagine that each wave that rolls in brings with it massaging and gentle relaxation and calmness. As the wave rolls out, it pulls along with it any tension that remains in your body. Scan your body. If you find any tension, let it go.

Massaging Relaxation

Go through your body once more, and relax even more until a very profound relaxation finds its place everywhere in your body.

Picture the ocean waves rolling in... and out with each breath. And with each breath imagine gently massaging relaxation flowing all over your body.

Picture massaging relaxation coming over and flowing around the top of your head. Feel the relaxation flowing into each part of the skin on your head and coming over the forehead and relaxing the eyes. The relaxation is entering parts of your eyelids and making your eyelids feel heavy and your eyes feel at rest, completely relaxed.

Now, the relaxation gently massages the rest of your face, and the feelings of relaxation move down to your nose. These massaging feelings of relaxation move over your nose and over your cheekbones and down through your throat and your mouth. These waves of gentle relaxation and massaging energy come one after another over your head and over your eyes. Your eyelids feel very heavy, and it's a very good feeling, a very relaxing feeling.

Let this relaxation move on down the back of your head and enter the very deepest muscles of your shoulders and neck. Feel the relaxation as it seeps into the muscles of your neck, relaxing each part of your neck. And as the muscles of your neck relax, the muscles of your shoulders relax, and the skin on your neck relaxes.

If you feel any tension, move your neck and shoulder a little bit until you feel more comfortable. Allow this relaxation to continue flowing over the shoulders to the upper arms and to the lower arms, coming down and relaxing the very deepest muscles of your arms. This relaxation pours down from your shoulders in waves of gentle massaging, over your skin, into your muscles, even into the flow of blood.

Every part of your body is becoming perfectly balanced, relaxed, and in harmony. It is flowing down over the shoulders into the upper arms, the lower arms, and through the fingers.

And, as this flow comes down from your head and neck, it also enters your back muscles, down through the neck into the back, so that you feel relaxation around each bone of your back and in all of the muscles in your back.

This energy continues through your stomach, into each part of your lungs, so that your breathing becomes low and quiet. You feel that all is well. Let it go down into the stomach and gently massage it, making it feel very heavy and warm.

Now down through the legs, the thighs, into the knees and the calves, and down to the feet and the toes. Feel wave upon wave of this relaxation pouring over your body.

Cue Words

Now, let's try to deepen the relaxation still further by using some cue words. Let's use the words "peaceful" and "calm,"

As you relax even further, think these words to yourself. Just say to yourself as you relax, "peaceful" and "calm," and then feel the deepening, ever-deepening waves of relaxation, as you feel much more peaceful and calm. Think of these words, these cue words, "peaceful" and "calm." Think very, very clearly about them as you say them over and over to yourself: "peaceful" and "calm."

Let the words echo in the back of your mind. Continue to relax and repeat the words "peaceful" and "calm" over and over again. In the back of your mind the words "peaceful" and "calm" echo over and over again.

Pleasant feelings of quiet have spread throughout your body. Feel your body and feel the calm. Let it relax fully. Feel at peace. Your breathing is regular and calm, calm and regular. You are now in a deep state of calm and relaxation. It is comfortable. You feel good. You feel refreshed.

"I am at peace." Say this to yourself. Feel the peace and the tranquility throughout your body. You will enjoy a good feeling every time you do these exercises, and you will feel more and more relaxed.

Return to Activity

If, during the rest of the day, or for that matter, if, at any time, you find yourself feeling upset about something, remember the relaxation you have just enjoyed. Before you get upset, take a deep breath and, as you breathe out, think the word "relax." Just think the word "relax" as you breathe out. Then for a brief period of time, think of the words "peaceful" and "calm," and let the feelings of relaxation that you are now enjoying come back to you. This will help you to control situations rather than being controlled by them.

Now, count from one to three. When you reach three, open your eyes. You will be relaxed, but you will be alert and refreshed.

One, relaxed, but alert...
Two, mentally wide awake...
Three, eyes open, alert, and refreshed...

Edward A. Charlesworth, Ph.D., is president of Stress Management Research associates and director of Willowbrook Psychological Associates, both of Houston, and on the faculty of Baylor College of Medicine.

Ronald G. Nathan, Ph.D.., is director of educational development, coordinator of behavioral science and associate professor in the departments of family practice and psychiatry, Albany Medical College. For eight years, he conducted the biofeedback clinic at Louisiana State University School of Medicine in Shreveport.

Both Drs. Charlesworth and Nathan have conducted stress management workshops for groups as diverse as homemakers, police officers, accountants, teachers, nurses, lawyers, secretaries, and dentists.

31

Entering Inner Space

Guide: Gloria Steinem

"Like the air moved by a butterfly, even your breath travels miles and links you to all things large and small."

Introduction

For many years, Gloria Steinem believed that concern with inner change was secondary to societal change. She saw, however, that the many gains made by women and men were not accessible to those with low self-esteem or addictions to authority and control. As she researched information for her own book to address these issues, she discovered that she, too, was lacking a sense of internal reality, which she addresses in *Revolution From Within*. This meditation in excerpted from that book.

In the early morning or other quiet time, take a half hour for yourself, find a comfortable chair that supports your back, and turn off the phone and other distractions. If this is impossible where you live, find a public library, religious space, or other quiet place for you (or for you and your partner) to absorb instruction like these:

The Journey

Sit with your back supported, feet flat on the floor, hands resting on your lap with palms upward.

Now bring your consciousness to one part of your body at a time, tensing each area as hard as you can, then just letting go. Feel the heaviness in each part of your body as you let it go — completely. Start with your toes... feet... calves... thighs... then the muscles of your torso... shoulders... arms... hands... then your face. Tensing each area — then letting go. Now feel your head balancing easily over your shoulders. Let your body center itself.

Inhale deeply and slowly. Feel your ribs expand and your belly push out as you slowly inhale — then exhale the air more slowly than you breathed in. Do this six times — with consciousness. Feel the cool air as you breathe it in and the warmer air as you breathe it out. Feel your body become larger with each inward breath and smaller with each outward breath.

Now forget about your breath completely and just feel the balance as you slowly close your eyes. Relax your eyelids, your forehead, relax your jaw. Let your mind "settle." If thoughts float up to the surface, don't resist them or pursue them. Just observe each one as it arrives — and then let it go.

Pause

Ask the back-of-your-mind to imagine a safe place. It may be a room you once knew or a place you once cherished. It may be a place you've never seen before except in this imagination of it — a beach, a mountaintop, a sunny room. As images come, trust them. If they don't come right away, just relax and wait. If they still don't come, imagine what a safe place would be like if you could imagine it.

Look around at this special place. What colors do you see? Run a hand over a surface near you: How does it feel? Are there special smells in this place? Are there tastes that seem part of this place? Can you feel the sun, the air, a breeze? What sounds do you hear? Notice which of your senses is the clearest or comes most quickly. Those are the strongest bridges to this safe place. You will be able to recall those feelings in everyday life when you need to feel safe. When you visit this place again, you may want to spend more time imagining with other senses and strengthening them, too.

Now just relax and be in this place. Nothing can happen here except what you wish to happen. If anything unwelcome appears, you will imagine it away. Only good things can happen to you here. Your unconscious is taking care of you. It has brought you to this special place of peace, restfulness, safety, and discovery.

Pause

Do you notice feelings? What is it about this place that makes you feel safe? Are there absences of things that give you that feeling? What other images, feelings, and associations do you notice? Let your conscious mind observe the gifts your unconscious is bringing you.

When your thoughts slip out of this place or you simply feel enough time has elapsed, you are ready to return. When you are back in your daily life, you will know that this place of peace and well-being exists within you. It will always be there whenever you need it. You will awaken feeling refreshed, centered, strong, and peaceful.

Inhale deeply and slowly as you count to six. Then exhale as you count to three. Do this several times — and feel the energy returning to your body. On the last count of three, open your eyes slowly. You have visited the home of your true self.

Gloria Steinem has been a writer and activist for almost thirty years. The author of two previous books, Outrageous Acts and Everyday Rebellions *and* Marilyn: Norma Jeane, *she is the consulting editor of* Ms. *magazine, which she co-founded in 1972. She also helped to found New York magazine, where she was its political columnist. As a feminist lecturer and organizer, she travels widely and also works for the Ms. Foundation for Women, a multi-issue women's fund, and Voters for Choice, a nonpartisan political committee. She lives in New York City, where her apartment is "a stop on the underground railway" for international feminists.*

32

Grounding

Guide: Carole Louie

"Find balance between your spiritual and earthly planes."

Introduction

For some being grounded comes easier than for others. We all feel the need to be grounded for one reason or another at one time or another. This exercise also works on objects as well as people. So if things are chaotic or in turmoil, try it and see if order is restored. For example, the first time I witnessed this exercise being performed was during a rough ride through turbulence on a 727. My next experience was to try it on myself. After a hectic three days of people needing my energy, it was my good fortune to sit next to a healer who ministered this healing imagery for me.

You can do this anywhere, lying down, sitting, or even standing up. Try to be as relaxed as you can, but don't worry if you feel apprehensive. This journey will help you find a more relaxed state, a more grounded state from which your perspective will be more balanced.

The Journey

Visualize the last bone of your spine — the tail bone. It is solid, although it has evolved to a very small bone. It is still firmly attached to the rest of the spine and exerts a downward pull just from its position as the last bone of your spine. Imagine that you tie a cord to this last bone. You know it is firm, but give it a little tug just to check that it is secure.

Let the cord fall to the ground, falling through the ground as it plummets toward the center of the earth. The cord is long enough to reach the center with just enough left to tie securely to an object there. So when you feel that you have reached the center of the earth, look for an object to tie the cord securely. It could be a branch or whatever you want it to be. Tug at the cord to be sure that it is firmly fastened.

The cord suddenly becomes more solid, like a pipe, and the diameter expands so that it is wide enough to fit comfortably under your hips. You have the feeling of being able to sit on it and of being firmly supported. Notice the texture, color, and firmness of the object. It may look and feel like a chair or bench, or it may just feel and look like a pipe. Take this time to know the object of support or grounding as you see it.

Breathe in deep breaths of golden love from the universe, and as you breathe out, let any worries, doubts, and fears you have accumulated move down the pipe or object at the end of your spine and down to the center of the earth. Breathe in and out several times in this manner and feel the release as the worries, doubts, and fears leave you and are replaced by the golden love from the universe.

When you have completed a total release, you are ready to move onto a higher energy.

Visualize a golden sun above your head. Let it expand and move through every part of your body. Let it fill your body until you cannot hold any more. Breathe in the golden light of the sun and the positive rays that it radiates. Know the unconditional love from the universal source.

When you are ready, completely filled with the loving golden sun's warmth and energy and full of love and peace and joy, open your eyes, shake your hands and head, and smile, letting your joy, peace, and love radiate to the world.

Carole Louie, A.S.I.D., is an interior designer in Naples, Florida. Her goal as a designer as well as a human being is to seek the outward expression of one's "interior" harmony and beauty as a way of life.

33

Lily Pad

Guide: Judith K. Bath

"By living in the moment, you are encouraged to move gently forward into the unknown and true growth."

Introduction

The peaceful, serene atmosphere of a cool pond, makes this an ideal meditation for relaxation. It can be especially helpful as a transition period between work and home or as tension release before beginning yoga or other exercises. It also increases feelings of self-acceptance, inner peace, and security. If practiced daily, your consciousness will expand to enhance this simple journey.

The Journey

Lie down and relax. Imagine that you are lying on a beautiful, green lily pad. The lily pad is just the size that you are. There is no room on the lily pad for anything but yourself. No room for thoughts or for doing... just room enough to "be." Just to be you.

You are lying on a lily pad in the middle of a beautiful blue pond. The pond is very still and peaceful. Let your body become heavy and sink comfortably into the lily pad. You are lying on your lily pad in the very center of the pond. Feel the space, the peace, the stillness... breathe in that stillness.

Surrounding the pond is a white sand beach with green palm trees. The sun overhead is filling you with warm, radiant light. Feel the beauty, the peace, and the energy.

A gentle breeze moves your lily pad like a small boat. You float toward one end of the pond. Notice a small opening. The breeze moves you along into a small stream. The current gently moves you along the water. Now, mangroves bridge each side of the stream. You feel safe and protected. Lazy clouds move overhead. Beautiful birds drift in the air currents. Breathe in the peace and the gentle energy of just being. Drifting down the stream, relaxed and appreciative of the energy and the peace. The gentle current guides you along your way. You do not have to do anything, just breathe and enjoy.

Gradually, the stream widens and comes into another large aqua blue pond. You float toward the shore. There are large trees along the shore, and they fan you with their branches. You are very, very comfortable. Enjoy the feeling.

The breeze becomes a little stronger and gently lifts you up onto the sandy beach. You can feel the warmth of the sand through the lily pad. The warmth is very healing. You feel part of the earth, strong and healthy. Breathe in peace, strength, health, and relaxation. Feel very quiet. Take the peaceful energy into your very center and remember it.

Now if it is time to return to your body and conscious thought... slowly becoming aware of your surroundings. Move your fingers and toes. Slowly, slowly open your eyes.

Remember the peace and the energy... and slowly come back to full awakeness. Remember all that was beautiful on your meditative journey and keep it in a place where you may access it when you need it. With renewed life force, continue on your activities.

Judy K. Bath has been a student and teacher of Yoga for twenty years. She has combined several styles to create her own style, which she calls "Gentle Yoga." She hopes her method will open doors and introduce students to a new and delightful path of spiritual, physical, and mental growth.

34

Progressive Self Relaxation

Guide: Joseph Ilardo, Ph.D.

"It's time to begin overcoming those fears."

Introduction

The following guided visualization was designed to help people achieve a state of deep relaxation before embarking on a series of "desensitization" exercises to overcome fear. This is the shortened form of the full length exercise contained in Dr. Ilardo's book *Risk Taking for Personal Growth*. It can be used at any time to bring on a state of relaxation.

The Journey

Settle back comfortably. Make sure that all your clothing is loose. Take a few comfortable, deep breaths. Stretch gently. Take another deep breath and let it out all at once. Close your eyes.

Focus on your arms. Take a breath, hold it, and tighten the muscles in your hands and arms. Hold the tension. One, two, three, four, five, six, seven. Now tell yourself to relax. Release your breath and let go of the tension in your hands and arms. Feel the difference between the tension and the relaxation.

Allow the warm current of relaxation to flow through your hands and arms. Allow it to swell and develop.

Pause

Now breathe in again. Hold it, and tighten the muscles in your hands and arms. Tighten. Hold. One, two, three, four, five, six, seven. Now all at once, release your breath and relax the contractions in your hands and arms. Study the feeling of relaxation. Breathe gently and comfortably as you allow it to flow up and down both arms.

Pause

Keeping your arms relaxed, focus your attention on your face. Take a deep breath and scrunch up your forehead and nose, while you press your lips together. Press. Hold the tension. Hold. One, two, three, four, five, six, seven. Simultaneously release your breath and let go of all the tension in your face. Relax all the muscles, and part your lips slightly. Allow all the tension to disappear. Feel the warmth flowing into your forehead and scalp. Allow the relaxation to develop.

Pause

Now breathe in deeply and tighten all the muscles of your face again. Tighten. Hold it. One, two, three, four, five, six, seven. Exhale and relax. Allow the relaxation to develop. Picture your forehead, and all the muscles of your face, as smooth and relaxed.

Pause

Now focus your attention on your neck, shoulders, abdomen, and buttocks. Take a deep breath and tighten all these muscle groups. Contract all the muscles of your trunk. Tighten. Hold. One, two, three, four, five, six, seven. Let your breath out all at once and simultaneously release all the tension throughout your central region. Allow all the muscles to relax. Study the contrast between tension and relaxation. Allow the warm current of relaxation to flow down from your face and throughout your neck... shoulders... abdomen... and buttocks. Once again, breathe deeply and tighten all these muscles. Study the tension. Hold. One, two, three, four, five, six, seven. Now tell yourself to relax, and let go of all the contractions at once. Feel the relaxation and comfort. Just let it flow and develop.

Pause

Now attend to your legs and feet. Keeping the rest of your body relaxed, take a deep breath and tighten the muscles of your legs and feet. Study the tension from your thighs, through your calves, and into your ankles and toes. Hold it. One, two, three, four, five, six, seven. Release your breath and relax all the contractions in your legs and feet. Breathe comfortably as you feel the absence of tension. Your legs feel heavy and limp. Allow the relaxation to develop.

Pause

Okay. Once again: Breathe in. Tighten your leg muscles, clench your toes into a fist. Hold. One, two, three, four, five, six, seven. All at once, exhale and release the tension. Breathe gently, easily, and regularly, and feel the relaxation travel from your hands and arms, across your face, through your neck and shoulders, and through your abdomen and buttocks, into your legs and feet. Enjoy the sensation of the warmth moving throughout your body. Notice how much you relax with each exhalation. Continue allowing these feelings of relaxation to develop on their own.

Pause

When you're ready, open your eyes. Stretch gently. Slowly get up, giving yourself plenty of time to adjust to moving about.

Joseph A. Ilardo, Ph.D., A.C.S.W., is a therapist in private practice in Danbury, Connecticut. He also teaches interpersonal communication, group dynamics, and public speaking at Lehman College of the City University of New York.

35

Sunset Sleep

Guide: Jule Scotti Post, M.S.

*"Now the sun is touching the horizon, and your body
is also sinking deeper and deeper into peace, into quiet."*

Introduction

I use this imagery for those who find it difficult to fall asleep.
Sometimes people take one or two hours to fall asleep. With
this sleep induction, they are often asleep within ten minutes
and sleep more deeply all through the night.

The Journey

You are lying in bed, feeling the pillow under your head and
covers around you. You may want to move around until you
feel completely comfortable. You can feel the weight of your
body as you sink down into the mattress. Your breathing is
smooth and deep, and each time you breathe out, you sink
down deeper into your bed, deeper into rest, deeper into
peacefulness.

Now in your mind's eye picture yourself sitting at the beach
in the west where the sun sets over the ocean. You can see the
red sun slowly sinking as streaks of pink and orange light up
the sky. The gray and purple colors of evening are spreading
darkness across the ocean, and you can see rays of pink and

gold reflected on the surface of the water. The seagulls have all flown away. The people who crowded the beach in the heat of the day have gone home. You are here alone in the peaceful quiet as the sun gets lower and lower. You can hear the waves rolling in and breaking on the shore. Now the sun is touching the horizon, and your body also is sinking deeper and deeper into peace, into quiet. Now the sun descends below the horizon until only the red-gold rim can be seen... sinking deeper, slowly deeper, until the sun is completely gone. Only a deep pink radiance glows above the ocean. And you too are sinking down, beginning to drift, to float, to flow into dreams of soothing ocean waves and deep restful sleep.

As you sink down into your deeper mind, your conscious mind may still be aware of sounds in the room around you while your unconscious mind is preparing a night of sweet dreams. Your conscious mind may still be aware of your head resting on your pillow, while at the same time your unconscious mind is inviting you to drift away into sleep. Your conscious mind may be aware of the darkness in the room and the quiet of the house. Your unconscious mind continues to take care of your welfare. Your unconscious mind is timeless and renews your strength and energy. Your unconscious mind releases all your concerns and cares and restores peacefulness and clear understanding. Your unconscious mind is ready to receive you as you sink down into a deep and restful sleep. And in the morning after a long night's rest you will awaken feeling relaxed and refreshed and alert.

Jule Scotti Post, M.S. is a psychotherapist working in a medical clinic in Maryland. She treats patients with chronic pain, stress and cancer using biofeedback, deep relaxation and group therapy. She has a Masters in Counseling Psychology and has training in group dynamics, guided imagery and music, meditation, Chinese medicine and hypnotherapy.

36

Thought Flow

Guide: Jean D. Stouffer

"Sometimes we must give up control to get it."

Introduction

So often our minds become a scramble of thoughts, a rampaging storm of "have tos" and "should haves" that overwhelm us and keep us frantic. This guided imagery gives us a quiet time to observe the process of how we contribute to the chaos in our minds. Once we understand the process, we can free ourselves from the demands of our thoughts. We can achieve a sense of inner stillness, and we can make decisions in a calm, quiet manner.

This is an excellent meditation for gaining some perspective on how our minds work. It can also be used during the night when the "have tos" and "should haves" interrupt our sleep.

The Journey

Begin by settling comfortably in a chair, your feet on the floor, and your hands resting quietly in your lap. Breathe easily and allow your eyes to close. Feel the support of the chair beneath you. You may want to shift your position a little as you allow your body to relax, becoming even more and more comfortable.

You can begin to shift your attention too. Notice your breathing... as you allow your breath to flow in and out... in and out. Nothing to do... no place to go... just the sensation of the air flowing in and the air flowing out.

As you continue to breathe comfortably, let yourself notice any areas of your body where tension exists. Allow your breathing to flow to these areas. And as you breathe out, allow the tension to flow out with each breath, just relaxing and letting go of any tightness. Let it go... breathing it out... releasing it into the air around you. Continue to breathe and release, breathe and release... no hurry... until your body is even more relaxed and free of tension.

Pause

As you continue to relax and breathe comfortably, you may find that thoughts intrude, thoughts of things to do or problems to be solved. You can learn something from these thoughts. Allow a thought to come in now, and grab it, really grab it and hold onto it. Hang onto it tightly. You may notice something. Notice how your body is feeling. Is it relaxed? Is it comfortable? Is your breath flowing comfortably and easily? Maybe you know something now that you didn't know earlier. Maybe you know a little bit more about holding on. So since you know about holding on, you can also know about letting go.

Allow yourself to focus on your breathing once again. That's right, the breathing... the air flowing in and the air flowing out... allowing your muscles to relax and your breath to flow calmly and peacefully. Breathing in and breathing out, comfortably. Nothing to do but just breathe and relax.

Perhaps you wonder if you could act differently when a thought intrudes. You can find out now. A thought is coming into your awareness. Do you see it? Good. But this time, don't grab it. Don't hold onto it. Instead, let that thought become something else. Maybe the thought will become a balloon on a summer's day, or clouds, or dandelion seeds drifting in the breeze. Maybe the thought will be a melody growing, then fading away in the distance, or a stream bubbling over rocks on its way to the sea. It can become whatever you want it to become. Just let the thought drift in and drift out, without holding on, without doing anything at all. Let it become something else, and let it go. Let it drift. And you can do this while you remain comfortable and relaxed.

You can even take some time to experience the flow of your thoughts, and you can do it now. As you remain relaxed and breathing comfortably, you can let the thoughts form, and then become something else. And that something else can drift out, floating gently by. There's just the drifting and the floating... coming... then going... here and gone.

Pause

When you are ready, allow yourself to focus on your breathing once again. As you become aware of the flow of air in and out, you may realize that your thoughts are a lot like your breath. Since you already know about holding thoughts and holding your breath, you can wonder where these new understandings will lead.

And you can let that thought float away, too, as you allow

yourself to become aware of your surroundings. You can begin to feel the chair beneath you, and hear the sounds in the room. Gradually allow yourself to become more alert, and when you are ready, open your eyes and return to your normal waking state, feeling refreshed, relaxed, and comfortable.

Jean Stouffer, a writer and a Certified Hypnotherapist (American Council of Hypnotist Examiners and Southwest Hypnotherapists Examining Board), currently practices in Albuquerque, New Mexico.

Inner Guides

37

Angel Introduction

Guide: Barbara H. Pomar, C.Ht.

"Angels... guardians... protectors... helpers.
They are there when you need them."

Introduction

Many of us have fallen in love with Angels at Christmas or remembered stories of Guardian Angels from our religious studies. They seemed like beautiful creatures... too beautiful to be just make-believe. During the '60s, I had the opportunity to meet and study Angels with Poleete in Los Angeles. Since that time, Angels have been an active part of my life — constant and reliable companions.

This introduction was designed to acquaint people with their unacknowledged angelic companions. For most people, their angelic companions are about as active as the Maytag repairman. These Angels are on perpetual "stand-by," and offer assistance when asked for it.

This guided imagery experience will help sensitize you to the awareness of the angelic kingdom around. The Angels have been around as long as you have, but we have lost the ability to communicate with them. Once people realize they have a very special being always near whose sole purpose is to help and protect, feelings of joy and confidence increase.

The Journey

Loosen any tight clothing and find a comfortable position. Relax as much as possible. Now, take a deep breath, letting your stomach stick out. Exhale the tension.

Starting at the feet, tense and relax each body part. Feet... tense and relax. Calves... tense and relax. Thighs... tense and relax. Buttocks... tense and relax. Hands... tense and relax. Abdomen... tense and relax. Chest... tense and relax. Shoulders... tense and relax. Neck... tense and relax. Roll your head gently side to side, forward and backward, around in a circle. Tense and relax your head. Take a deep breath and feel the brain and all the muscles in the brain and head relax.

Imagine a shaft of sunlight shining down on you. Feel its gentle warmth all around you. Imagine the light is a protective shield, allowing only love, light, and goodness in and reflecting anything negative or hurtful.

Now, inhale the white light down the spine, way down. Exhale... expanding the white light out. Be aware of the various energies around you: sounds... smells... lights... colors.... Identify each. Acknowledge each. Give thanks for each.

Now, inhale the white light down the spine, way down. Exhale up the spine through all the energy centers, which some people call chakras. As you exhale imagine various colors flashing... red, orange, yellow, green, blue, indigo (navy blue), and purple. See them form a perfect ball of white light over the top of your head.

Expand that ball of light around you. Inhale the light. Exhale through your heart with love. This light, your personal energy field, is your love that you communicate with other beings. Acknowledge the other beings. Give thanks to the members of the angelic kingdom who assist with those qualities of the physical world. Realize that non-physical beings may have properties that are not familiar to us physical beings.

Mentally welcome your Angel into your light. Thank your Angel for being there. Ask to see it... to perceive it. Listen. Listen for another energy source... a voice or sound of perception that is not yours... one that may sound a little different. Sense. Feel... the presence of another being... a lighter, finer energy mass. See. Use your sense of perception. What does this being look like? Pay attention to details. It may have a particular color, shape, or sound. It may speak with music or in tones within your heart... quietly, loudly, softly, or angrily. Leave the censoring until later. Acknowledge with gratitude whatever you sense, see, feel, or hear. Listen, and as you do, the communications will improve.

Introduce yourself.... Ask its name, what it prefers to be called.... Listen in your heart. What comes to mind. This might seem to be imagination. Allow these thoughts, this dialogue. Often times, when the dialogue stops, the communication begins. Don't censor it at this point. Afterward, you can compare the information, the dialogue, to what you know is right, just, and fair.

What does your Angel want to say to you at this time. Any message?

Pause

Thank your angel. Ask if there are any other messages or information that may be beneficial at this time....

Pause

Your Angel offers you a gift.... Take it. Thank your Angel. Look at it. What is it? What comes to mind when you see it, touch it, feel it? What is your Angel saying about it?

Pause

Tell your Angel you'll see them/him/her again.

Take a deep breath into the body. Feel energies returning and circulation increasing even better than before.... Feel healthier and better than before. Start moving... returning fully present... feeling better than before. Stretch... retaining all you have heard and learned. Open your eyes. Sit quietly or make notes for a few minutes.

Barbara H. Pomar is a Certified Hypnotherapist (American Council of Hypnotist Examiners) in Salisbury, Maryland, specializing in hypnotic and non-hypnotic regressions (past, present, and future.) She leads seminars and workshops nationwide in meditation, past-lives, and dreams.

38

Inner Voice

Guide: Geneva B. Mitchell, D.C.H.

*"You may be surprised to learn that this
amazing power is part of you."*

Introduction

Through listening to my "inner voice," my unconscious, I
was able to create this imagery. It helps acquaint a client with
this "inner" part of himself or herself. It is best tape-recorded
and practiced privately or with a friend.

The Journey

Take a long, deep breath and close your eyes. Breathe deep
and long. As you listen to this voice, it becomes more
soothing, and you become more relaxed. Any sounds you
hear other than this voice are distinct and clear, you focus on
any sound, other than my voice; the clock, traffic, children
playing, or airplanes. Focus on any sound other than the
voice.

Allow those sounds now to fade away, farther and farther
away, until for whatever reason, now you only hear the voice
and perhaps the music. You now hear inner messages.
Whatever you are hearing is what you most need to hear; so

while you listen closely or not, you will be assisted in ways best needed by you to give you the answers to problems. But it's up to you. The answers you want are available here.

Now we will go on a marvelous, quiet adventure. With your closed eyes, take easy breaths and imagine that you are standing on a path. This path leads to adventure and beauty; so begin to slowly become aware of standing on the path. Look to see what you are standing on. Is it sand or gravel? Perhaps, it's grass or stone. Begin walking and be aware of any sounds. Perhaps you hear only stillness at first, and then slowly the sounds of insects and birds come into your awareness. And as you begin to look around, you see tiny insects, butterflies, ants going about their business. Look over there, under a bush and see a spider spinning a shiny web that sparkles in the sun. Feel the sun inside and around you.

You feel so good as you wander down the pathway and continue to notice the sounds around you. You also become aware of smells. It seems to be citrus, perhaps lemon or maybe orange. You step around a corner and find that you are at the edge of an orange grove, and you recognize the strong smell of orange. It's pleasant and you like it. You pick an orange and bite into it; it's sweet as it runs down your throat. As you continue to walk, you seem to float along under the trees. It's quiet; it's sweet; the air is clean as after a rain. You feel light and airy, as if you can float anywhere you like, and that is just what you do. You float up into the air. Now you are looking down on the pathway and the orange grove. The day becomes still as you drift up into the atmosphere. It's very still, only the wind is here with you. Now the still wind sings melodious chimes like a wind chime — wonderful and peaceful. The clouds are clean; there is pureness; you are free to drift, float into space — safe, connected, no feeling. You are slowly drifting along down into the softness. A spot appears, and you drift into a cozy space. A comfortable space wherever you are, wherever you choose.

Now you see clearly where you are; you are peace, freedom, tranquility. Notice the lightness, airiness. Notice where you are, what you see and hear around you, what you smell, breathe in slowly, deeply, slowly and deeply. Now just be. Relax in a place where the energy is the greatest for you, doing what you want to do and watching miracles being accomplished. Make a commitment to trust yourself and notice how everything in your life changes rapidly, gets better and better, sooner and sooner.

In a little while, your eyes will open or you'll just sleep; either is okay. You make the choice. It's fine. The music leads you to awareness or sleep. Let it happen.

Geneva B. Mitchell is founder and director of New Image Hypnosis Center in Albuquerque, New Mexico. She is a dedicated, motivated hypnotherapist with many interests such as writing and public speaking. She has recently published a book entitled Take The Power This: Life is Yours.

39

Meeting Spiritual Guides

Guide: Chrystle Clae

*"Lovingly relinquish your negative
emotions and memories."*

Introduction

One of my own Native American guides wrote this meditation through my fingers in a blessing for a meditation class
that I was teaching. Many people comment on the sense of
comfort and belonging that remains following this imagery.
Use it as often as you wish. You may wish to develop and
name the guides, so that you can call upon her or him
whenever you wish.

The Journey

Imagine you are standing in front of a fire. Look deeply into
the fire — breathe deeply, and as you breathe deeper notice
the fire growing larger. It is not a fire that is capable of
burning you.... It is a Divine Fire of Illumination. Breathe
and gaze even more deeply.

Begin to sense an intelligence in this fire.... Within this
Divine Fire is your most aggressive guide. This guide is loving
and gentle, but you have south out her or him to aid you in

burning up any stubborn negativity in your present life — to make way for new, fresh, and productive growth that she or he can direct to you.

Your guide want you to bring to mind some area of your life that still needs purging, releasing, cleansing. It could be a relationship in which you need to forgive or make amends, a habit that you want to release, a negative aspect of your life that needs to be cleansed. Take a moment and form a picture of what it is your guide can aid you in purging....

Take the picture or strong feeling you have chosen and place it in this purging fire.... I is handled lovingly by your guide because no matter how negative it is, it has been a teacher to you in some way... but now you are ready to be free of it — to go on. Watch or feel as it is cleansed by the flames and your guide offers it back to the universe to be utilized in a productive way....

Now feel the bond between you this loving guides. Ask you guide to give you some sense of direction. You may ask for guidance of how to use this purging for your most productive growth.... Take a moment and be aware if your guide shows you a symbol... a scene... a sound... a feeling... a word that will help you to understand the next step on your spiritual path... a step that will affect your everyday life as well....

Gaze once more into the fire and know that this guide will continue to communicate with you through your dreams and meditations and in bringing new people and lessons into your everyday awareness!

Breathe deeply and come back gently to this room.

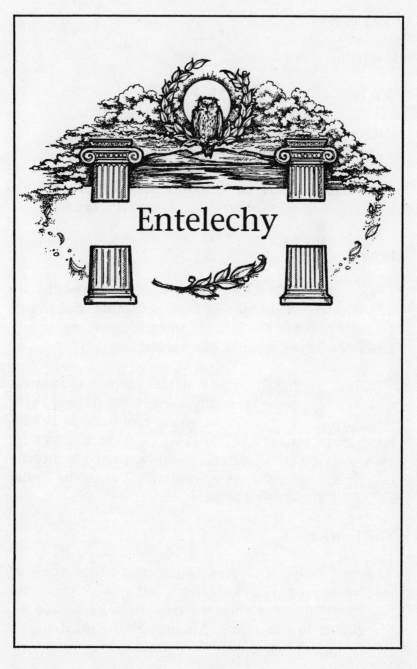

Entelechy

40

Linking®

Guide: Marti Glenn, Ph.D.

"Our beliefs shape our reality and color — if not spawn — all our thoughts, feelings, and behaviors."

Introduction

The Entelechy Process is a cybernetic feedback spiral that can help you understand and heal hurtful situations that arise in your everyday life. Entelechy is Aristotle's word that simply means the actualization of one's potential.

"Linking" is designed to take you from a current situation in which you experience strong undesirable feelings, back through similar situations in young adulthood and child-hood to the earliest scenario in which these feelings were present. With this discovery, you'll gain some immediate insight and can continue to work with it using the "Inner Messages" guided visualization.

The Journey

To begin, think of a recent situation, perhaps one that involved a partner or close friend, that evoked strong, un-pleasant feelings and which you'd like to understand better. The guided visualization will begin with the situation you choose and move back through three previous situations. This usually begins with the current scenario, goes back to young adulthood, then adolescence or grade school, ending at a very early time. Of course, there is no right way to experience this. If what emerges for you is different, go with it. If nothing emerges, simply sit with the feeling you're experiencing in your body and be curious about what will emerge.

Begin by assuring your privacy and making yourself as comfortable as possible. Take a few deep breaths and exhale with a sigh.... Allow your eyes to close when they're ready.... Allow your breath to begin breathing you.... Watch it rise... and fall.

Pause

Imagine yourself now in a very relaxing place, any special place you feel tranquil.... As you're relaxing there, begin to find yourself drifting back to a recent situation where you had strong emotional feelings, or the scenario you want to explore now.... Allow yourself to be in that situation. Notice every detail: where you are... what you're wearing... who's with you.... Notice also, if there's music playing or other sound... any particular aromas or tastes.... Engage all your senses....

Pause

See or imagine the other person in the situation as clearly as you can, beginning to replay any conversation as if it were happening now. If it's more appropriate, you might imagine someone else there to hear you.... As the words come, allow the feelings to emerge in your body.... Notice where you carry the feelings, and for the sake of this learning, see if you can intensify the feeling.... Notice also if there are other words that need to be spoken or actions taken as you continue to experience the feelings in your body even more....

Pause

Continuing to stay in touch with the feelings, release the situation now and allow the feeling in your body to take you back to a younger time when you felt a similar way, perhaps earlier in your adulthood. The circumstances may have been different, but the feeling was the same.... Notice what situation emerges and again, be there with all of your senses.... Notice who is with you and what you are feeling.... As the scenario unfolds, bring the feelings into your body even more.... Say the things that need to be said here....

Pause

Stay with the feeling in your body and allow it to take you back now to an even earlier time, perhaps in adolescence or grade school, when you have felt a similar way.... The circumstances may be very different, but the feeling in your body will be the same.... As this situation emerges, deepen the feeling, and begin to speak to the other person about how you're feeling.... Continuing to say whatever needs to be said, whether the words were actually spoken at the time or not....

Pause

Saying good-bye to that situation now, and staying in touch with the feeling, allow the feeling in your body to take you back to the very earliest time you might have experienced it. Remember, the circumstances may be very different, but the feeling in your body is familiar. Just focus on the feeling in your body and allow it to take you, then notice the first thing that pops into your mind, even if it doesn't make complete sense. Just follow it and let your imagination fill in the details.... Notice where your parents are and what they might be feeling.... You may want to invite your feelings to intensify... and then allow your adult self as loving ally to slip into the scenario....

Pause

Notice what the child's inner voice is saying about herself or himself, what belief is beginning to form.... Knowing this, spend a few moments completing anything that needs to happen with the child or the ally.... Stay here as long as you need to.... Whenever you'd like, say good-bye in whatever way feels appropriate....

Pause

Begin to bring yourself back when you are ready, sensing your surroundings... stretching and moving... and making notes in your journal as appropriate.

41

Inner Messages

Guide: Marti Glenn, Ph.D.

"To change beliefs, we must access the unconscious mind since that is where the beliefs reside."

Introduction

Inner Messages and the other meditations in this series can provide specific tools for deep and lasting change. After practicing these meditations, many people are able to respond differently to situations that once caused anxiety or emotion pain.

Use the "Inner Messages" guided visualization to discover the beliefs and decisions that you made as a child that still affect your life now.

The Journey

Select an early memory you would like to explore, perhaps the one you discovered in the "Linking" process. Have your journal or paper handy for taking notes when the visualization is complete.

Make yourself as comfortable as possible.... Take yourself to a peaceful place.... As you are relaxing there, begin to find your body going into a warm, heavy, sleepy state while your mind becomes more and more alert.... In fact, your arms and legs are feeling as though they almost couldn't move and your mind is taking this opportunity to sharpen its observation skills.... Your mind begins to float above your body and watches as you sink more deeply into the relaxed state.... Your mind becomes more curious about a particular scene from your childhood, and you find yourself floating back to that early experience you have chosen to explore.... See if you can float toward this childhood scenario, watching from a distance, and recreate it with all of your senses.... Notice where the child is and who else is there.... Listen for any sounds... and breathe in any aromas.... Notice colors and textures.... Begin to observe the child in the situation.... Notice the child's body, the way she or he is responding to what is going on.... See if you can tell what the child is feeling — both sensations and emotions....

Pause

Imagine now that you have a special receiver and can discern the child's self talk. You can hear what this little one is saying inside about herself or himself.... And you can know clearly what the child is beginning to believe about herself or himself. Perhaps you hear something like, "I'm not very smart; There's something wrong with me; I'm bad; I'm unlovable or I'm helpless." Just notice what the beliefs are, what is being said....

Pause

Listen now for what the child is telling herself or himself about other people or the outside world. Perhaps you hear something like, "I can't trust them; This is not a safe place;

They know more than I do; They're O.K. but I'm not."
Whatever the beliefs are, notice them as they arise....

Pause

Next, begin to watch the child's behavior and see what she
or he is deciding to do in order to stay safe and have his or her
needs met.... Spend the next few moments simply watching
the child in this situation, noticing feelings, beliefs and
decisions, observing how this child is shaping his or her life
in order to feel secure, to have basic needs fulfilled and to be
accepted or loved....

Pause

As you are ready, allow yourself to come back to the peaceful
spot where you have been resting and begin to feel your body
and sense the space around you.... You may want to make
some notes about the feelings, beliefs, and decisions that
emerged for the child from this situation. You may do this
before or after you bring yourself back to full waking consciousness.

42

Re-creation®

Guide: Marti Glenn, Ph.D.

"Recreating old beliefs is the single most important thing you can do to empower yourself and create the life you want."

Introduction

"Re-creation Meditation®" is used to heal the child and re-create the beliefs. When you uncover beliefs and decisions that were made in childhood and change them to beliefs that are more appropriate for you now, you will find your everyday life going more smoothly. You will begin to experience more freedom, joy, and personal power. You will move ever closer to your Entelechy.

This guided visualization is designed to help you heal old wounds and re-create old beliefs that are no longer appropriate so that these false beliefs no longer run your life. You'll need to select an experience you want to re-create, usually, but not necessarily, an early memory. This can be an actual memory from imagining yourself as a child in a particular situation. It is helpful to first have done an "Inner Messages" guided visualization so you can work with beliefs that you have already identified. It is also helpful to have your journal nearby so that you can make some notes about your experience when you complete this process.

The Journey

Assure your privacy and make yourself as comfortable as possible. Take a few deep breaths and exhale with a sigh.... Allow your breath to begin breathing you.... Watch it rise... and fall.... You may find now, that each breath can take you deeper and deeper into this relaxed and peaceful state.... Imagine yourself almost drifting or floating to a very special place, one where you can relax and be yourself.... As you relax there, begin to find yourself drifting back to the experience you want to re-create.... See if you can allow yourself now to become the child.... Notice where you are and who is with you.... Engage your senses as much as possible, sensing all your surroundings: seeing, noticing colors... hearing sounds... noticing any interesting aromas... any textures, like what you're wearing and what's around you.... Notice how you, as the child, are feeling in this situation.... Become aware of your body and how these feelings manifest.... Notice especially your breath, perhaps your stomach, back, or heart.... Just allow the situation and the feelings to emerge within you.

Pause

Allow yourself now to be at once the child and also become an ally for the child: a loving adult who understands and can see the entire situation clearly.... You're the child and you're also yourself as a loving adult.... Demonstrate to the child, in whatever way seems appropriate, that you understand the situation, you can see what's going on here.... Show the child that you understand her or his feelings.

Pause

You might want to thank this little one for making a decision that kept you safe, that really served you during your growing-up years.

Pause

Help the child to see that the beliefs she or he holds about herself or himself are not accurate: the beliefs that say "I'm not O.K.; There's something wrong with me; or somehow I'm bad." Gently help the child to know these assumptions, these beliefs, are really *not* accurate.

Pause

Help the child to re-create a belief that *is* accurate, that *is* really true, that she or he is really O.K., she or he is lovable and capable.... What is the belief that *is* true about this little one?

Pause

Now, help the child redecide. That is, decide to be another way. It's really no longer necessary to behave in a certain way in order to survive or to get your needs met. There is greater understanding now and more resources are available. So, help the child develop a new decision, a new way to be in the world, a new way to be with herself or himself.

Pause

Notice that sometimes, if the child is in a very toxic environment, it may be necessary to remove her or him to a safer, more loving place. Decide as the ally what's needed in this situation for a new belief and a new decision.... And notice if there is anything this little one needs to say to you or you need to say to her or him for now.

Pause

It's time to say good-bye to this little one for now, with a thought that you will return when it's appropriate,.... or if it's necessary, you may bring the child with you.... Whichever you choose, look this little on in the eye and reaffirm the new belief. For example, if the new belief is "I am a lovable person," call the child by name and say, "You are a lovable person." That is to say, "I see you as who you really are.'

Pause

Also affirm the new decision, which might be telling the child, "And now you can be this way," or whatever that is. Really see and affirm what is true for this little one, now.

Pause

Experiencing how this feels in your own body as the adult, turn, look beside you and notice there's a future version of yourself, a wonderful old woman or man, perhaps seventy or eighty years old or older, vibrant, smiling. Realize that this is the future you who's learned who she or he really is. This Wise Being knows how to be in the world and is here to be with you, as your ally. So spend a moment together, listening to the decisions and beliefs that this Wise Being has for you. Whatever needs to be said or done, allow it now.

Pause

Noticing how it feels to be truly understood, allow your Wise

Being now to look deeply into your eyes, calling you by name, really seeing you, and affirming what is true about you... that you are worthy, lovable, and capable... you're fine just the way you are... or whatever the new belief is... whatever your new Truth is.

Pause

Breathe this in and notice how it feels in your body. It's often a little scary at first to hear the real truth about yourself, that in the deepest core of your being, you are whole. Breathe now and receive the Truth.

Pause

You might notice if your Wise Being has a name or if there is a way she or he likes to be called, because this wise and loving part of yourself is now available to you any time you need support or a little wisdom....

Say good-bye to your Wise Being for now, knowing that the two of you may return here at any time. In fact, both of you may want to go back to the little child as allies at some point.... But for now, bring yourself back with a feeling of who you are with this new belief, this new Truth.

For just a moment, project yourself experiencing this Truth, into the next few days, into your relationships... your work... or other situations.... Imagine yourself there now.... Notice how your body feels believing this about yourself, perhaps behaving in a new way.... Stay with this feeling of who you really are; know your Truth, and breath it in as long as you care to....

Allow yourself to stay in this place as long as you like.... When you are ready to return, begin to feel the room around you.... Stretching and moving... bring yourself slowly to full waking consciousness.... Staying with this feeling, make some notes in your journal about your experience, about what you know.

It is important that over the next few days you continue to affirm your Truth. It is also very helpful to write this new belief on a small card or Post-it Note and place it where you will see it several times a day. As you go to sleep each night, in that deeply relaxed state, reaffirm your Truth and when you awaken in the morning, invite your Truth to go with you during the day. You may find that as you do this, your life is more and more just the way you want it to be.

Marti Glenn, Ph.D. is an author, psychotherapist, and former professor of counseling psychology. She is co-founder and Director of the Entelechy Institute, Santa Barbara, California. For the past two decades she has been actively involved in research, teaching, and practice in the fields of brain/mind psychology, human potential, peak performance, and psychotherapy. She has written and recorded dozens of guided visualizations and facilitates workshops, including Entelechy, throughout the United States.

Training & Skill

43

Removing Blocks
to Success

Guide: Janet Dean

"Release the blocks that take the power out of your success."

Introduction

This visualization was created for a "Success Workshop" to help participants overcome events that may have been keeping them from fulfilling their destinies. Seeing a traumatic or disturbing event as a cartoon with make-believe characters will help you experience it from a new perspective and free your mind to picture success.

We all fear success much more than failure, but often we don't know why we won't allow ourselves to express our unlimited potential.

Sometimes viewing a serious event through a cartoon scenario takes out the scariness. I learned this when I helped an incest survivor change the frightening picture in her mind to a cartoon because it helped remove the fear surrounding the event.

The Journey

Sit in a comfortable position. Place your feet flat on the floor or cross them at the ankles. Place your hands on your lap, open ready to receive. Take a deep breath... in through the nose and out through the mouth. Relax. Take another deep, deep breath. Relax. Relax. Relax. Take another deep breath and picture yourself in front of a movie theatre. The theatre is an old one, large and ornate with a big marquee in front. On the marquee in huge letters are the words "Success Story, The Story of _____," and there is your name. And then to your surprise it says *starring* and there is your name again! Marvel at the sign and gaze at it with pleasure. You decide to enter the theatre and see this movie about *you* starring *you.*

You look around the theatre, but you can't find an empty seat. An usher appears in front of you and says, "We've been expecting you. Your seat is down in front." You follow the usher down the aisle until you come to a seat that looks like a throne. It is velvet in your favorite color, and it suits you perfectly. The usher invites you to sit on the throne and puts a stool under your feet. He says "Your wish is my command" and stands at your left shoulder.

The curtain opens and you see a beautiful scene. There is snow on the ground with a brook running through. You hear the sound of the brook. What a peaceful sound. As you look at the relaxing picture and hear in your mind the running water, the usher speaks. His voice is calm and quiet and full of love. He says, "Sit back and relax." You wonder, "How?" Reading your mind, he says, "Picture a ray of pink light coming in the top of your head and swirling around your body relaxing as it goes... down through your neck, into your shoulders, down both arms. Feel your arms become limp as the ray travels up your arms and down through your chest, stomach, and to the other organs. Now the ray goes down your legs. Feel your legs become limp and your feet tingle.

The pink ray travels back up your legs, back up through your chest and neck and out your head taking all your negativity with it."

You feel very relaxed, but the usher says "You can relax even more. Please follow my directions. Picture yourself standing at the water's edge." You see yourself there as soon as he says it. He continues, "Picture yourself walking alongside the brook until you see the water begin to course down a hill. As you watch the water flow downward, you will feel at one with all life, and you will become more deeply relaxed. I will count from ten to one. When we reach the count of one, you will be completely and deeply relaxed. Ten, relax, go deeper... nine, relax, go deeper... eight, relax, go deeper, seven... relax, go deeper... six, relax, go deeper... five, relax, go deeper... four, relax, go deeper... three, relax, go deeper... two, relax, go deeper.... One. You are now ready to view the movie."

The curtain closes, and the usher says "Remain relaxed, it will just be a moment." The curtain reopens, the screen is revealed, but it is blank. The snow scene is gone and so is the brook. The usher speaks, "Think of a time when you felt less than successful. It could be in your childhood, or your teenage years, or your young adult years, or right now. If there is one experience that you feel is holding you back, use that incident. See yourself on the screen and involved in the action that affected your feelings about yourself. How do you feel? Scared? Angry? Guilty? Envious? Or some other emotion?

"Realize that this is just a movie you are watching; you cannot be hurt. If at any time you feel uncomfortable, breathe deeply and bring yourself back to the here and now. Let's go on.

"Continue to look at the screen. As you watch, the screen changes, and the scene you've been watching turns into a cartoon. Again it stars you."

The usher pauses and waits for you to catch up. Seeing you are ready, he goes on, "This is a cartoon of your original problem. Using whatever cartoon figures you like, see them reproducing the experience that you had, but his time, laugh at the antics of the cartoon characters taking the power out of the situation. Imagine happy music such as merry-go-round music in the background, and feel yourself becoming more joyous and light-hearted. You are in the cartoon, and since you can make yourself look any way you want, be the way you always wanted to be. You are in charge of how your movie goes just as you are in charge of how your life will go. See the cartoon showing you successful, feeling good about yourself, enjoying who you are, doing everything you wanted to do and being joyful doing it." The usher pauses while you savor the scene. The screen goes blank.

The screen again lights up, and you see yourself as you are today doing something you always wanted to do. Maybe it's writing or painting. Maybe you want to own a business or work in a different field. Perhaps you want to go back to school or ski or sky dive. Only you know what the secret desire is that your fear of failure or success has held you back from pursuing. Are you fulfilling that desire now? Are you doing what you have been afraid to do? Is it exhilarating, exciting? Are you glad you're doing it? Do you feel more confident and joyous? Remember you are now the director and the producer of your movie as well as the star, so you can make any changes you want.

The usher speaks, "See how successful you can be when you

let your fears go. I am well-pleased. Now you know you are a winner, and it's time you received a reward. You are going to present yourself with a trophy." The usher hands you a three-foot tall trophy made of pure gold and shining brightly. Written on it is *Congratulations, You Are a Winner,* and your name is right below it. He tells you to walk up to the screen where the *screen you* is smiling, happy that you have done what you have feared to do for so long. As you reach toward the screen with the trophy, the *screen you* reaches out and takes it from you smiling a thank you. You breathe a sigh of happiness and go back to your seat. How blissful you feel. Success is joy-producing and since success breeds success, you know with certainty that you can do anything you want to do in all phases of your life.

Applause breaks out. The usher touches you on the shoulder, and you know the time has come for you to leave the theatre. You arise from the throne and go up the aisle followed by the usher. You notice for the first time that the audience is made up of your family, friends, teachers, co-workers and anyone who has touched your life. Some of these people have in the past been part of your problem, but now they are a part of your victory. You smile and wave to them all knowing they can't hurt you anymore. You are now confident within yourself, and you walk up the aisle feeling yourself slowly coming back to the here and now. The usher shakes your hand and says, "Congratulations." For the first time you notice the usher looks just like you. You say thank you and leave the theatre feeling wonderful knowing the usher will be guiding you forever.

Janet Dean and her husband, Ken, facilitate A Course in Miracles in group, and they are graduates of the Silva Self-Mind Control method. They enjoy sharing their learning and helping others enjoy the journey of life.

44

Nature of Resistance

Guide: Jacquelyn Small

"{Learn} to work with resistance, not against it."

Introduction

Use this exercise when resistance is present in your own life or in the therapy session. Resistance will also be present in the processing. Work with the resistance, not against it. And drop the content of the personal work that created the resistance until you are clear on what the resistance is. Study this exercise carefully before attempting to use it.

Transformers do not abruptly press themselves or persons they guide past a point of resistance. They view resistance as a gift to be respected. They do believe, however, that it is their obligation to help discover where the resistance is coming from, in themselves as well as in others.

Give the person you are guiding permission to resist, even to hold up on processing. (Most often, this permission will paradoxically cause them to want to talk about the experience.) When processing, be sure to help the person ascertain whether the resistance was from the higher or lower self.

The Journey

When you sense resistance, begin by pointing out to the person you're guiding (or to yourself) that you are perceiving their objections as resistance. Ask the client what it feels like. If she affirms that it is indeed some sort of blockage to a particular aspect of personal work, ask them if she would like to explore where the resistance is coming from.

Explain that it can be a message from her lower self, having its basis in fear. Or it can be a message from her higher Self, as a way to step down her energy, which the higher Self senses is moving too rapidly. In order to determine from which unconscious mind the block is being constructed (the subconscious or the superconscious), the Transformer asks the client or friend to close their eyes and breathe a while (to relax the body). When you feel they are somewhat relaxed, say: "Now, very spontaneously, allow an image to come into your mind that symbolizes your resistance...."

When she has a symbol, ask her to describe it in detail. If the symbol is representative of anything that is down, heavy, dark, or thick, it will be from the subconscious (fear-based). Examples: a dark wall with no windows, black mud covering the entrance to something, heavy weights bolting a door, a "No Exit" sign beside on spelling "Danger." Sometimes the subconscious images will be shadows, murkiness, thick, dark clouds, or amorphous substances that block our vision.

If, on the other hand, the image is one from the higher Self, it will be one of a master, a teacher, guide, or Christ figure, usually robed in white, or beautiful or aged, representing strength, purity, or wisdom. Or often it will be a symbol of a cross, a rose, a serpent encircling a staff, a crown, a field of green grass, a brilliant light, or some type of religious symbols. It will be white, golden, yellow, or shades of blue, violet, or rose. All of these are symbols from the superconscious mind, the home of the higher Self.

If the subconscious is blocking, ask the person you are guiding if she would be willing to talk about her fear. See what guarantees she would need for safety or comfort in order to proceed. If she resists, let it go. (If the pattern is significant, you can bet the issue will resurface again.)

If the superconscious is blocking, tell her to respect her higher Self's wishes and follow its guidance. It knows more about what's better for her than you do. If your client asks you why her higher Self would be blocking a piece of personal work, you can share with her the knowledge that her higher Self (for some reason) knows she is not ready yet to deal with this particular issue in life. Perhaps it would require certain moves in her circumstances that would adversely affect innocent persons. Or it might give the client or friend too much to deal with right now, which might produce discouragement on the path, or some kind of breakdown.

Jacquelyn Small, M.S.S.W., author of Becoming Naturally Therapeutic *and* Awakening in Time, *has touched the lives of thousands in the innovative workshops and lectures she conducts throughout the U.S. and Canada. She currently serves on the advisory board for the national Council on Codependence. Her company, Eupsychia Inc. is a healing and training center dedicated to bridging traditional and transformational psychologies.*

45

Door

Guide: Tom Kenyon

"The images that this technique generates can be profoundly moving and insightful."

Introduction

The purpose of this visualization is to assist the user in gaining knowledge and insight about a particular problem or area of interest. It uses imagery that the unconscious mind immediately understands.

The first step is to decide what information or insight you want. Form your area of inquiry very clearly in your mind before proceeding.

The next step is to make yourself more receptive to the images and feelings that will arise from this process. You will do this with something called Level One Breathing to slow down your brain waves thus increasing alpha and theta activity. Such activity is associated with increases in mental imagery and dream-like experiences.

Exercise

Level One Breathing

1. Inhale to a count of 8 (each count is about 1 second).
2. Hold breath in to a count of 8.
3. Exhale to a count of 8.
4. Hold breath out to a count of 8.
5. Repeat the above sequence 7 more times for a total of 8.

Repeat Level One Breathing until you have a comfortable "floaty or spacey" feeling.

The Journey

Now imagine and sense that you are standing in front of a door on the other side of which is something literal or symbolic having to do with your question. You may see the door or simply have a sense about it. Neither way is better than the other. Just go with the way that seems most natural to you.

Imagine that you are placing a hand against the door and sense the "energy" or feelings coming from the other side.

Now open the door and step into the other side. Look around the space and notice what is there. It may be immediately apparent what the object or being means in relationship to your inquiry. Or it may be somewhat obscured.

You may communicate with this object or being as if it were in a dream. Simply direct your question to this object or being and allow yourself to receive its communication. You may hear it speak to you or you may have a feeling or simply a knowing.

(Note: You may wish to do another cycle of Level One Breathing at any time you feel yourself "coming out" of the experience. Just breathe according to the directions given earlier and then return to the visualization after you have completed the breathing protocol.)

Tom Kenyon, M.A. lives in Shelton, Washington, and holds a master's degree in Psychological Counseling from Columbia Pacific University. He is the founder and director of research and development for ABR, Inc. (Acoustic Brain Research) a leader in psychoacoustic research. Psychoacoustics is the study of how sound, language and music affect the brain and human behavior. He is also the originator of Body/Mind Re-education™ a form of rapid transformation used by therapists and counselors. Mr. Kenyon conducts human potential trainings in both the United States and Asia.

46

You Can Visualize

Guide: Betty Perry

"Enjoy the moments; they are the best times you have."

Introduction

Many people feel that the process of visualization is like having a three dimensional movie screen in your mind. For some this is true. For others when they close their eyes, all is black. A better term for the process we call visualization would be Mental Sensing. In the following exercise you will use all of your senses at the mental/spiritual level. Just as you use all of your senses at the physical level, you also use these same senses at your inner conscious levels.

The Journey

To begin this exercise find a comfortable sitting position, close your eyes and take a deep breath. Exhale slowly, and as you do, feel tensions and tightness drifting away. Continue to breathe slowly and deeply; with each breath you feel a warm relaxing feeling flowing slowly downward throughout your entire body.

Pause

Allow your breathing to return to normal as you enjoy the feeling of being relaxed and comfortable.

From this relaxed state let us begin to explore our mental senses. The sense most relied upon is our sight, and we will begin there.

SIGHT: Call to mind a Christmas tree, a fire engine with lights flashing, a sunset, a yellow flower, a sunrise, something shiny, trees covered with snow.

SOUND: How does a car horn sound? Rain on the window? A dog barking? Thunder? The Star Spangled Banner being sung? Keys rattling? Your stomach growling?

SMELL: Call to mind the smell of freshly baked bread, the smell of coffee brewing, smell of gasoline, of rain, of a rose, of a banana, of wet paint.

TASTE: How does a fresh crisp apple taste? A lemon, a pretzel, vanilla ice cream, peanuts, your favorite beverage, hot soup, a pickle, peppermint?

TOUCH: Imagine holding a cold wet sponge, a piece of sand paper, a mug of hot soup, a piece of velvet, a squirming puppy, a sleeping infant.

Now imagine that you are standing on a hilltop on a warm summer day, there is a stiff breeze blowing, you are drinking lemonade and looking at a rainbow.

You have just experienced how you use all of your senses at the mental or spiritual level. This is what the process of visualization is for you.

It is now time to return to an awake, aware state. Take a deep breath and as you exhale slowly and gently open your eyes. Relaxed, aware and awake.

Which sense was most fully experienced? The least? Whatever your experience was, this is how you process information in your mind, often referred to as visualization.

Betty Perry of St. Petersburg Beach, Florida, draws her experience from a varied background in nursing and business when presenting the Silva Method and other motivational and developmental seminars.

Freedom & Awareness

47

One with Earth

Guide: Annette Covatta

*"Awaken to the collective consciousness formed by
the thoughts of every human being."*

Introduction

This visualization was inspired by the pictures of the planet
from outerspace and the subsequent realization of the
interconnectedness of all living beings on the earth. It helps
bring us closer to a sense of unity — at–oneness — with all
creation and offers us a challenge to be responsible toward
effecting a viable future for all life on this planet. Use this
visualization when you are feeling isolated, disconnected, or
adrift from the movements of the earth.

The Journey

Gently close your eyes. Let go of all conscious thoughts...
thoughts that have a quality of busyness about them, that
tend to grip you, control you. Let these things drop away.
You have no other place to be, nothing else to do but to *be
here* now... in this place, in this moment.

Feel your body weighted toward the earth. Feel the earth's
vibrations spreading through your body... to the tips of your

fingers... to the crown of your head. Feel the tingling of warmth and energy through your body... your toes... your fingers... your genitals... your scalp. Then, return your attention back to the connecting point where your body meets the ground of the earth. Let a sense of peace and quiet permeate your whole being....

Know that you are the vital connection between the ground of the earth and the sky of the universe!

Now, bring your attention to your breath... Let each inhale of breath fill your body with the earth's atmosphere. Let each exhale give back to the earth a cleansing nourishment. Stay in this rhythm of your breath....

Know that your life-breath movement of inhale and exhale is at one with the gentle, balancing life-movement of the earth... like the rise and fall of the wind... like the wings of birds in flight... like the gills of fish in deep waters... the swaying of trees... the ocean waves rolling in and out. Stay with this sensation... the air of the earth, filling your lungs... the breath of your body, swelling the earth.

As you sink deeply into the swaying of your breath, you become aware of a glistening, golden thread floating in front of you. You cannot see where it begins or ends. You reach out to touch it. At the point of contact, the golden thread widens into a carpet. You feel your body weightless even as you are drawn forward, riding on the golden carpet, lifting you up and out, farther away from the earth into the vastness of space. You feel perfectly safe, free, and expansive! The gold shines and sparkles brighter and brighter as the space around you becomes blacker and blacker. All movement stops. Your body sinks comfortably into the soft, silky texture of what has now become like a flying saucer transfixed in space. All is quiet, and the silence is beyond all human experience.

You look around you... above... below you. Blinking dots, far off, like huge, glistening diamonds... the moon aglow from the rays of the sun. Then your eye catches the ineffable wonder of the round earth shimmering with dazzling swirls of blue and white, speckled with browns, greens and vibrant slivers of raspberry! Of a sudden, you feel part of an unbroken continuum with no sense of separateness. Like a raindrop at one with the sea, you are awakened in your being... in your consciousness.... You are at one with the earth.

Now the soft, golden carpet begins a slow, gentle descent down to the earth. The carpet is supported by a soft wind. It begins to turn into a color of luminous green like the greening of springtime... like the lush green of the original, untouched rainforest. You float down on the fresh, moist, green carpet. You feel safe... protected... as if by a consciousness of knowing and loving that pervades all space and time. The green carpet ripples its way closer and closer to the edges of earth.

Now you have entered the earth's atmosphere, moving through clouds and floating above, close enough to notice meadows, rivers, mountains, and gardens. When your feet touch the ground, you are encircled by children and adults... all shapes and sizes... different skin colors... diffcrent sounds, smells and speeches.

You feel a depth of connection with each one like never before! The oneness moves beyond the sense of human family, enfolding into the circle everything on the earth... animate and inanimate things... every cell in your body as well... the undivided wholeness of all things... all part of a single consciousness, an all-knowing intelligence... beyond comprehension! You sense that you are seeing things differently.

You ask yourself, "What is this different way of seeing?... of being? What does it feel like?... How will I live on this planet beginning now and into tomorrow and the future?"

Let yourself rest now, sitting on a large rock in front of you... perhaps pondering these questions... or just being where you are, in a daydreamy state. A poet's image washes over you:

> To see a World in a Grain of Sand
> And a Heaven in a Wild Flower,
> Hold Infinity in the palm of your hand
> And Eternity in an hour.
> *William Blake*

And now, in your own timing, when you are ready, return to the room, feeling refreshed, energized, peaceful, and loved.

Annette Covatta, D.M.A., has a lifetime involvement in the arts and personal growth programs, and she holds a Doctor of Musical Arts from Boston University. Ms. Covatta is the founder and director of FULCRUM, an organization whose mission is to enable persons to reach their potential through the body/mind/spirit/soul connection. Through FULCRUM, she presents workshops which reflect her interest in the creative process and holistic spirituality.

48

Oneness

Guide: Larry Moen

*"This is a learning process to develop
beyond our own limitations."*

Introduction

The experience of "Oneness" with the creative source of all
energy, is possible when we find ourselves without emotions
that are too high or too low. To discover unconditional love,
the true force that dwells deep within each of us, and to
accept the world without judgment. We extend our arms and
our hearts to show respect for all that surrounds us, for all
that is within us — for whatever we perceive as bad or good.
Often we choose a path of resistance before we are open to
return to the Source. But that is O.K. This meditation was
created to help you express and enjoy the feeling of Oneness
that many of us seek. Remember you will be armored with
love for protection as you travel the path before you. Begin
to realize that our lives are of little importance in the scope
of the vast and unfolding universe. Be one with who you are
and use this imagery to see life as it was truly meant to be
seen. See beyond your own concerns and know that loving
Energy is all that matters in this existence.

The Journey

Find a comfortable position, preferably lying on your back with your eyes closed, your arms by your side, palms up, and your feet uncrossed. Direct your attention to feeling directly from your spiritual heart, which is located in the center of your chest. A warm, wonderful, loving feeling from the spiritual heart begins to expand with each breath, flowing in and out of each organ, each body part, every muscle, and bone. This glowing sense of love spreads around your skin and then surrounds your whole body with warmth and love.

Absorb the love and sense its energy surrounding every cell in your body.

Begin to see yourself rise up, as though you are floating detached from your body. Stand back a little and look at yourself from a different angle. Look down at yourself visualizing your entire body as it begins to change.

Visualize your body as having the consistency of fluid with a gel-like solidity. Your body, your clothes, your hair, and your jewelry are all resilient.

Now imagine, if you pushed your body, it would shake like Jell-O. Visually place your finger on any part of your body and watch what happens. Watch how your skin and your clothes and your hair are all pushed in, and when your finger is withdrawn, they snap back into their original position.... Let this form soften a bit and turn into a dissolved gelatin, any color gelatin that you would like. The gelatin is similar to a thick liquid, that of peach juice, pineapple juice, or nectar juice. Now imagine placing your finger in any part of your body and swirl it. Watch what happens.

Pause

Remove your finger and watch the elements go back into shape just as they should. Watch the gelatin liquid turn into a finer liquid, one which has less body, like soda, any kind of soda that you choose. Bring your attention back into your body and feel the carbonated bubbles in your back and moving up the back of your legs, the back of your buttocks, and the back of your head. The tingly little carbonated bubbles are moving upward in your body. Just experience that feeling.

Pause

Float above your body again and in your mind's eye, place your finger in the soda and stir it around... pinching your fingers together. Pinch your hair and see how it dissolves, just as soda water would. And when you let go, it reforms the hair and becomes again what it was.

Now further dilute the soda. Eliminate the coloring and the carbonation from the soda. Visualize yourself as pure, colorless water. Look at your face and the curvatures of your face. You are pure fluid. You look almost like a liquid ice sculpture, except you are not ice. You are liquid. Reach down and scoop up a handful of any part of your body. Dip your whole hand into your body. What does it feel like? Is the water cold or is the water warm? Now cup your hand and pull it out as you hold a handful of water. See what happens.

The water falls from your hand back into your body. The remainder of the water falls gently between your fingertips. Notice each drop reforms your clothes, hair and skin; they all blend together again. The last drop splashes into your body and instantly reforms to its original shape....

Direct your attention to your feet where you open an imaginary valve and let the water flow out slowly. See it pouring out of your heels in gentle waves.... As it drains, you see a vague mist where your body was. You have become air. Giving yourself permission, inhale a single breath and float up toward the sky, soaring like an eagle, higher and higher, gliding through the air. You have become air and now become one with everything. Enjoy this wonderful flight, floating upwards dissolving into space.

Pause

It is now time to return. You may float face up into your body. Allow the water to return, allow the water to fill your entire being... your clothes and your hair are water again. Now become the soda. Notice the carbonation tingling in your body. Bring in the heavier mass which is the gelatin. Notice the color of the gelatin as it turns into the resilient form, just kind of floppy and bouncy. Visually push your body a couple of times and see what happens to remind yourself how it bounces back into shape.

Allow your conscious mind to be aware of your body again. Thank your wonderful mind for giving you the opportunity to take this journey.

Now remember the love and affection that flowed into your body and let it continue to absorb into your being. You have the ability to draw from that heart energy at any time you wish. Feel yourself now in your conscious body. Wiggle your toes and move your legs, shake your arms, make fists, and then relax. When you are ready, open your eyes and be aware, as never before of the life force around you. Know this is the life force in all of us.

Inner Child

49

Embracing Your
Lost Inner Child

Guide: John Bradshaw

*"The unresolved grief work is a re-experiencing process
liberating and integrating your lost inner child."*

Introduction

This meditation has been used by John Bradshaw as a
powerful conclusion to his workshops on liberating the lost
inner child. "Toward the close of the workshop, I have each
participant encounter his Lost Child. I cannot describe the
power of this exercise...." Below is a written outline of the
meditation, which according to Bradshaw, is extremely
powerful when used through a tape recorder. Bradshaw
recommends using Daniel Kobialk's "Going Home" as background music.

The Journey

Sit in an upright position. Relax and focus on your breathing... spend a few minutes becoming mindful of breathing...
Be aware of the air as you breathe it in and as you breathe it
out... Notice the difference in the air as it comes in and as it
goes out. Focus on that difference... (one minute).

Pause

Now imagine that you're walking down a long flight of stairs. Walk down slowly as I count down from ten. Ten... (ten seconds) nine...(ten seconds) eight... (ten seconds), etc. When you reach the bottom of the stairs, turn left and walk down a long corridor with doors on your right and doors on your left. Each door has a colored symbol on it.

As you look toward the end of the corridor there is a force field of light... Walk through it and go back through time to a street where you lived before you were seven years old. Walk down that street to the house you lived in. Look at the house. Notice the roof, the color of the house and the windows and doors... See a small child come out the front door... How is the child dressed? What color are the child's shoes? Walk over to the child... Tell him that you are from his future... tell him that you know better than anyone what he has been through... his suffering, his abandonment... his shame... Tell him that of all people he will ever know, you are the only one he will never lose. Now ask him if he is willing to go home with you?... If not, tell him you will visit him tomorrow. If he is willing to go with you, take him by the hand and start walking away... As you walk away see your mom and dad come out on the porch. Wave goodbye to them. Look over your shoulder as you continue walking away and see them getting smaller and smaller until they are completely gone.... Turn the corner and see your Higher Power and your most cherished friends waiting for you. Embrace all your fiends and allow your Higher Power to come into your heart.... Now walk away and promise your child you will meet him for five minutes each day. Pick an exact time. Commit to that time. Hold your child in your hand and let him shrink to the size of your hand. Place him in your heart... Now walk to some beautiful outdoor place... Stand in the middle of that place and reflect on the experience you just had... Get a sense of communion within yourself, with your Higher Power and with all things.... Now look up in the sky; see the purple white clouds form the number five.... See the five become a four... and be aware of your feet and legs... See the four become a three... Feel the life in your stomach and in your arms. See the three become a two; feel the life in your hands, your face, your whole body. Know that you are about to be fully awake — able to do all things with your fully awake mind — see the two become a one and be fully awake, remembering this experience.

John Bradshaw, author of best-selling Bradshaw On: The Family *and television host for the PBS series of the same name, was born in Houston, Texas, and was educated in Canada, where he studied for the Roman Catholic priesthood, earning three degrees from the University of Toronto. For the past twenty years, he has worked as a counselor, a theologian, a management consultant, and a public speaker.*

50

Welcome the Child

Guide: Louise L. Hay

"It doesn't matter how old you are, there is a little child within you who needs love and acceptance."

Introduction

Most of us have ignored our inner child far too long. One of the core issues that we want to begin to explore is healing the forgotten child within. Every age that you have is within you — within your consciousness and memory. As children, when something went wrong, you tended to believe that there was something wrong with you. No matter what your early childhood was like you, and only you, are in charge of your life now. If your mental images of the past are strong and you keep affirming, "It's all their fault," you stay stuck. Use this meditation to develop a new relationship with your inner child.

The Journey

Put your hand over your heart. Close your eyes. Allow yourself not only to see your inner child but to be that child. Let your own voice speak for your parents as they welcome you into the world and into their lives. Hear them say:

We're so glad you came. We've been waiting for you. We

wanted you so much to be part of our family. You're so important to us. We're so glad you are a little girl. We love your uniqueness and your specialness. The family wouldn't be the same without you. We love you. We want to hold you. We want to help you grow up to be all that you can be. You don't have to be like us. You can be yourself. You're so beautiful. You're so bright. You're so creative. It gives us such pleasure to have you here. We love you more than anything in the whole world. We thank you for choosing our family. We know you're blessed. You have blessed us by coming. We love you. We really love you.

Let your little child make these words true for it. Be aware that every day you can hold yourself and say these words. You can look in the mirror and say these words. You can hold a friend and say these words.

Tell yourself all the things you wanted your parents to tell you. Your little child needs to feel wanted and loved. Give that to your child. No matter how old you are or how sick, or how scared, your little child needs to be wanted and loved. Keep telling your child, "I want you and I love you." It is the truth for you. The Universe wants you here, and that's why you are here. You've always been loved and will always be loved throughout eternity. You can life happily ever after. And so it is.

Louise L. Hay, a metaphysical teacher and bestselling author of nine books including "You Can Heal Your Life," has assisted thousands of people in discovering and using the full potential of their own creative powers for personal growth and self-healing.

51

Your Child of the Past

Guide: Gloria Steinem

*"No one... knows the experience, feelings, and
needs of your inner child. Only you do."*

Introduction

Self-esteem is created in childhood, but as Gloria Steinem
relates in her book, *Revolution From Within,* "It's never too
late for a happy childhood."

"Meeting one's inner child," she says "is an experience both
common and unique.... Reentering the past as your own
protective parent doesn't change it, but it can *change your
emotional response to past events."*

The Journey

Take a moment or two to be aware of your feelings about
today's adventure. Are you fearful of this meeting? Or eager
for its discoveries? Is this child a familiar part of you, or
someone you've tried to forget? The emotion is less important than your ability to feel it.

Allow an image of your inner child to float to the surface
from that back-of-the-mind. Trust whatever comes: a shad-

owy figure, an image from an old photograph, a version of the child you've never seen before, an infant, a teenager, a little child who runs to you, one who ignores you or turns away.

Before you reach out to this child, ask yourself what emotions she or he evokes in you. Do you feel happy or ashamed? Angry or impatient? Indifferent or affectionate? Awkward or at ease? Judgmental or accepting? Once you have sensed this, ask another question: "Am I feeling this way toward my inner child because my mother, father, or other caretaker felt this way toward me?" If so, take some time to understand that you did not invent this feeling, it was given to you. It isn't yours. It can be changed. Stay with these thoughts for this first meditation or come back to them for as long as you need.

Pause

Invite the child to be with you — but respect the child's response. If she or he isn't ready yet, that's fine. Explain that this is a special place where you do only what you wish. Your inner child may have been forced to pretend in the past, and it's important that this doesn't happen here. Try waiting until the child speaks to you — and if the child isn't ready yet, just stay there quietly and observe this child of the past. There will be a next time. There's plenty of time.

After the child does talk or come to you, see if he or she would like to be hugged or to sit on your lap. Feel the warmth and weight of the child's body, its contrast in size with yours, a small hand in your hand, the texture of skin and hair. Take a moment to be aware of the emotions this evokes in you — and in the child.

Pause

If the child comes to you easily and is open and happy, you might say: "I am your friend from the future. I'm here because I love you. I want to learn from you.'

If the child is shy, unhappy, or afraid, you might say: "I've come from the future to help you and love you. I will protect you. Just tell me what you want and need.."

At any point along the way, one of you may sense that you've come as far as you want to for today. That's fine. Assure the child that this special place will always be here. Whenever you need it. If the child is troubled or lonely, you might leave a part of yourself to comfort the child — and tell him or her that you are doing this. If the child has a spontaneity or other qualities you feel you have lost, you might ask a part of the child to stay with you after you return.

As your time together ends, remember that whatever you have thought, learned, or felt here is now part of you. The child is also part of you. You will come to know, trust, and help each other.

Take some energizing breaths, inhaling slower than you exhale. Count to six as you breathe in, count to three as you breathe out. On the last count, open your eyes. Look at your hands, and imagine that a child's hands are inside them. You are one and the same person — but different. You can protect and care for your inner child.

Don't forget to make notes of your thoughts, impressions, associations, and feelings.

Gloria Steinem has been a writer and activist for almost thirty years. The author of two previous books, Outrageous Acts and Everyday Rebellions *and* Marilyn: Norma Jeanc. *she is the consulting editor of* Ms. *magazine, which she co-founded in 1972. She also helped to found* New York *magazine, where she was its political columnist. As a feminist lecturer and organizer, she travel widely and also works for the Ms. foundation for Women, a multi-issue women's fund, and Voters for Choice, a nonpartisan political committee. She lives in New York City, where her apartment is "a stop on the underground railway" for international feminists.*

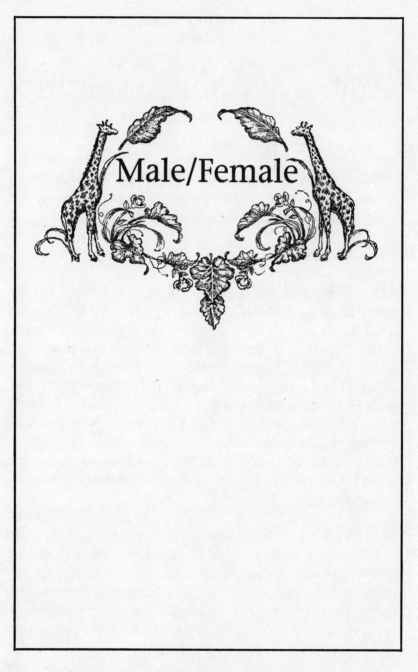

Male/Female

52

Archetypal Shape-shifting

Guide: Jean Houston, Ph.D.

"Identification with these [archetypes] in one way or another has proven essential to the practice of sacred psychology in many places and times."

Introduction

The extension of the kinesthetic body and imaginal body into the mythic realm allows you to prepare for the exercise that follows. In the imaginal-body exercise, you experience(d) reality from the perspective of different animals and perhaps different mythic personae, and you moved from place to place in the physical realm. Here we enter more explicitly the realm of myth and archetype, using the skills you have gained in working with the imaginal body. Now you will learn to engage, with a more expanded imaginal experience, both god identities and archetypal perceptions. These are yours for the having, since they live just below the surface of consciousness.

If you do this exercise carefully, you may notice a considerable change in feeling and perception as you move from one archetypal identity to another. The genius of the shapeshifter within you can be used with as many additions and variations as you like, to enrich the perceptual-conceptual continuum of your own knowings. To have such empathy with archetypes is not only to gain the eyes of Athena, the taste buds of Dionysius, or the tactile sensations of Aphrodite. It is to release oneself from the perspectives of local space-time; it is to gain the ideas of gods and prepare oneself for the rigors of therapeia.

The Journey

Sitting comfortably and relaxing totally, follow your breath for the next few minutes, all the way in and all the way out. With each breath cycle let your local identity become more porous and permeable. Allow yourself to be in a state of leaky margins so that you can more readily experience the godselves that are waiting to be assumed.

Now let there rise in you from the imaginal realm the archetype of the Great Mother. Feel the body and being of this archetype stream in your own being, so that you find yourself becoming the Great Mother. Now move in the body and being of the Great Mother. Know what it feels like to move as the Great Mother and then look out at the world with her compassion and senses and knowing.

Pause

Now release the Great Mother and let there rise in you from out of the imaginal realm the archetype of the Wise Old King. Feel the body and being of this great archetype enter fully developed into your own being, so that you find yourself becoming the Wise Old King. Now move around as the Wise Old King and know what it is to look out at reality with the responsibility and the perspective of the Wise Old King.

Pause

Now release the Wise Old King and let there rise in you from the realm of imaginal forms the archetype of the Young Redeemer. Let yourself become the Young Redeemer, feeling his energies and form stream into you so that you do not know where you begin and he leaves off. Move as the Young Redeemer. Know the world as the Young Redeemer knows it. Even sing as the Young Redeemer.

Pause

Now release the Young Redeemer and let there rise in you from the imaginal realm the archetype of Dionysius, the god of wine and of intoxication, of excess and too-muchness. Let the fullness of body and the sensory appetites of this god fill you to the brim. Laugh and snort as Dionysius, reach for the ripe grapes, drink deeply from life's many pleasures, and know yourself as Dionysius.

Pause

Now release Dionysius and let there rise in you from the imaginal world the archetype of the Great Snake. Let yourself receive the sinuous twisting form of this archetype, your voice becoming a hiss, and your mind a mystery that remembers all earth magics. Move and be known as the Great Snake.

Pause

Now release the Great Snake and let there rise from the imaginal world the archetype of the Trickster. Let yourself become the Trickster, with his subtle form, his movements like quicksilver, his mercurial disposition. Now, filled with whimsy and mischief, consider what you as Trickster can do to the reality around you.

Pause

Now release the Trickster and let there rise in you from the realm of the imaginal the archetype of the Holy Child. Let that little body move into yours, and feel yourself as that small, that complete, that innocently wise. Wholly becoming the Holy Child, look out at reality with the innocence, wisdom, and grace of this archetype.

Pause

Now let your own local identity return to you, quickened by the knowing that you are a One who contains the Many. Know, too, that each of these great symbolic figures, as well as many other, dwells within you and can be engaged deeply and felt imaginally, granting you access to both their perspective and some of their capacity.

Individuals may want to discuss and share the archetypes they discovered, or they may want to sit quietly with music playing as they reflect on their capacity for archetypal shape-shifting.

Jean Houston, Ph.D., a pioneer in human development, internationally renowned scientist and philosopher, and past president of the Association for Humanistic Psychology, has conducted seminars and worked in human development in more than thirty-five countries. She is director of the Foundation for Mind Research in New York and is the author of more than ten books.

Excerpted from The Search for The Beloved, © *1987. Reprinted with permission of Jeremy P. Tarcher, Inc., Los Angeles, CA 90069.*

53

The Goddess Within

Guide: Mary Ellen Carne, Ph.D.

*"Learn to tap into the universal energy of
the Feminine Principle that is available to all who seek it."*

Introduction

The purpose of this guided imagery is to use the metaphor of
the Goddess to help women experience the energy of the
Female Principle that is within the core of their being.

It also assists women in finding that universal source of the
feminine energy and in maintaining a connection with the
essence of their female qualities and self. It is a wonderful
meditation to practice regularly or to experience as a group.

The Journey

Relax, deepen, and surround yourself with protective light,
a white light that surrounds your body and mind. Know that
this white light is a symbol of spiritual protection and as
such, will screen out negative influences while allowing
positive thoughts and feelings to enter. Each breath you take
allows you to experience this protection from the white
light....

If you wish, take a few deep, cleansing breaths, breathing

218

from your center and allowing the awareness of this process to bring you more deeply within yourself. Let each breath remind you that it is your center which nourishes you, and it is your breathing that takes you there.... Letting yourself sink deeper and deeper into relaxation, feel each breath you take as a source of energy as well as relaxation. Allow your breathing to move you deeper and deeper into yourself, all the while protected by the white light that surrounds you....

You are moving down into that center place of knowing, floating down into the sacred place of the Great Mother, the Female Principle, the Deep Feminine within you... floating and moving downward until you find yourself on a beautiful, deserted, tranquil moonlit beach. Here on this quiet beach, radiantly lit by the moon, you sit for a moment and watch the moon beams sparkling and shimmering across the dark, still water. The sparkling beams dancing on the fathomless waters carry you even deeper into your reverie.

Pause

You rise now and begin a slow, steady walk, winding your way along the shoreline with your path guided by the iridescent moon. It is as though the light of the moon is drawing you to an ancient, sacred place. You feel an irresistible pull that draws you toward it, just as it once pulled our foremothers to the sacred temple of the Goddess. They would go to this sacred place for rituals of healing, dreams of prophecy, and celebration acknowledging the divinity of their being, bringing regeneration and rebirth to their female spirit....

Now you too, like ancient women, have the opportunity to enter this sacred temple to encounter her energy, to see her divine essence reflected within yourself, and allowing you to recognize your own divinity as woman. The Goddess throughout the ages appears in many forms and in many ways through dreams, a vision, a spark of intuition, in nature, or through creative inspiration. This ancient energy of the Goddess appears to serve as a catalyst to awaken divine energies from within women, energies that continue to flourish and flow in their consciousness long after they leave this sacred place....

Find yourself now, where recently only a few have journeyed, in the time and place of the ancient civilizations of the Goddess now buried and nearly forgotten. It is a place of joy, of serenity and peace, a place of wholeness, balance and wonder, and a place that honors the essential power of woman.... You are pulled along, pulled as the tides are pulled by the moon, drawn back into the time when the Female Principle was revered, an age that is past, present, and future all in one....

Pause

Slowly, in this place you now find yourself, the outline of a majestic temple appears before you. Move closer and closer until you find yourself within the sacred temple, however it appears before you. This is a temple beyond the reaches of time, a temple that is the sacred space dedicated to the Goddess, the Female Principle, The Great Mother energy within you.... Beams of moonlight enter the temple to show you the way into the inner sanctuary of Self. You enter with reverence and anticipation.... You have now arrived in the most sacred place, a place found within your center. This is the domain of the Great Mother Goddess. This is her "home" within you. You receive a real sense of the divine energy that rests here. Spend a few moments opening and creating this space within you; once again allowing her entrance, elated that you are able to return to her in this way. Honor and accept whatever comes, a mixture of radiance and darkness, embracing all, for all of her is sacred and divine.

Pause

Now allow yourself to rest in this space and, just as our foremothers of ancient civilizations did, have a dream — a dream of healing, of renewal, of rebirth for yourself through the Goddess. Take a few moments to fully experience this empowering dream of her energy and your own divinity reflected through her....

In your dream, form a picture of her or a symbol or sensation of her, using all your senses... seeing, hearing, tasting, touching, smelling and knowing.... What is she or her energy like? How does she feel about you? How is she like others you know? Does she have anything to say to you? Create a vivid composite of the fullness of her energies, both light and dark, positive and negative. Receive the gift of this moment and experience her as fully as possible, creating her energy and image using every sense available to you.

Pause

Now feel yourself being wrapped in all of the qualities you perceived as though you are being surrounded by her energy or being held in her arms. Sense and receive the healing she brings to women who are open to her possibility....

And now find yourself gradually awakening from your healing dream, allowing your experience to become less intense, fading slowly into the background of your consciousness.... Find yourself returning to the inner sanctuary of your sacred temple. You are able to see it once again, only this time with a much deeper and profound sense of knowing of the energy that rests here — a knowing of the essence of the Goddess, The Female Principle... a knowing of yourself as a woman of divine essence. You recognize that you have received a deeper understanding of the sacredness of the Female Principle within you, a new vision and sense of being female that extends far beyond the limits of your cultural image. All has been manifest to you through your Goddess dream. Celebrate this gift of knowing, celebrate this dream and this sacred place, and celebrate your being there and your Being divine....

Slowly bring yourself back to the room, allowing the divine female energy you have discovered within yourself to replenish, restore, and inspire you. Find a way, in your own time, to comfortably leave this experience, knowing that you can return there whenever you wish just by moving to that deep center place within you.... Slowly, slowly, gently and easily move yourself back and up to your usual waking reality. Taking your time and remembering all that you have experienced. Come back refreshed and energized by your journey and when you return to the room, open your eyes, stretch your body and be fully present.

Mary Ellen Carne is a "Female Principle" educator and masseuse and Stress Management Consultant. She enjoys supporting and sharing personal growth journeys using a psycho-synthesis methodology. She has developed workshops and classes including, "Intuition and Imagery," "Women and Mythology," "Wisdom Within — Self Discovery Through Myth," "The Female Principle," and "Unearthing the Goddess."

54

Healing Our Sexuality

Guide: Karen Carnabucci

"Open the way to healthy expressions of sexuality with this imagery."

Introduction

This imagery was created for an outpatient counseling group. Many of the participants had suffered sexual abuse or been raised without adequate information concerning sexuality. The damaging effects of sexual abuse by others or the "shaming" messages from parents or caretakers about sexuality can be explored and released through this imagery. Many clients have been able to connect with long-suppressed feelings and to learn to validate their rights to healthy expressions of sexuality. It may be helpful to process this information with the support of a trusted friend or therapist.

The Journey

Relax... feel yourself as an adult in your childhood home. Stand at the door of your bedroom as a child.... Walk in and see yourself as a child sitting alone on the bed. Notice how that child is dressed, how his or her hair is fixed or cut, and the expression on the face of that child. Sit next to the child and hold your child safely and securely. Look into your child's eyes now, and feel yourself becoming that child.

Pause

As the child, recall a time when you felt shamed, humiliated, embarrassed, angered, fearful, or punished because of your sexual curiosity, behavior or questions.

Pause

Perhaps you recall a time when your body was used or exploited without your permission or understanding.

Pause

See yourself and hear yourself telling your adult now about that incident and what it felt like for you, at the time it happened and today as you recall it.

Pause

As the adult now, look into your child's eyes and tell the child that you hear those feelings. Validate the child and tell the child what will affirm the child in a safe and loving way — that it's all right to be curious, that it's all right to ask questions, that it was wrong to be exploited or forced into unwanted activities, that he or she is safe now, or whatever else the child needs to hear.

Pause

Then give that child an affirming hug, and as you do that, give yourself a hug right now, wrapping your own arms around yourself.

In your mind's eye, open your eyes to see that your child self is now an adolescent, perhaps twelve or thirteen — the age when body changes are beginning to take place — or perhaps slightly older, when you are more of a young man or young woman....

Notice how your adolescent is dressed, how his or her hair is cut or arranged and the expression on the adolescent's face. As you find yourself looking into your adolescent's eyes and feel yourself becoming that adolescent....

Remember a time as an adolescent that you felt shamed, humiliated, exploited, confused or fearful about your sexuality....

See and hear yourself explaining that incident and your feelings about it at the time and talking about it today.

Pause

As the adult, give yourself an opportunity to take in that message and then validate this young person and tell him or her what will affirm him or her in a safe and loving way — that he is safe, that it's normal to have questions about sexuality, that it's normal to experience body changes and develop, that it was wrong to be exploited, used or forced to participate in unwanted activities, or whatever else your adolescent needs to hear.

Pause

Then give your adolescent self a firm hug of affirmation, again by wrapping your arms around yourself....

When you open your eyes in your mind's eye, you see that your adolescent self has disappeared, and you are now in your own bedroom at home.

When you are ready, get up and walk to the mirror in this room and look directly into your eyes which are reflected to you in the mirror. Think of a time when you, as an adult, have had difficulties with an issue or experience relating to your sexuality.

What did you say to yourself then? What do you need to say to yourself now? Speak to your adult self now, and tell yourself what you are willing to do to affirm your sexuality on a daily basis, a weekly basis, a monthly basis.... Tell yourself that it is all right to be a sexual person with sexual needs and desires; that you have a right to express your sexuality in a loving, caring, and appropriate way; that if difficulties continue to be present in your life, you have a right to seek competent and professional guidance, and say whatever else you need to say.

Pause

Become aware of the floor beneath your body, be aware of the sounds of music in this room, the sound of this voice. When you feel ready, open your eyes. And when you feel ready, sit up, and return to this room.

Karen Carnabucci is a therapist specializing in experiential thera-pies, including psychodrama, family sculpture, and imagery, in her work with adult children of alcoholics and dysfunctional families. A former newspaper writer and editor, she is a consulting therapist at Caron Family Services, an internationally recognized drug and alcohol treatment center in Wernersville, Pa. She recently collaborated on a book, Intimacy, The Quest for Connection.

Children's Visualizations

55

Accepting Myself

Guide: Maureen Murdock

*"It is our job as parents and educators to
make children feel safe and secure in who they are."*

Introduction

A healthy self-concept exists when we accept who we are, exactly the way we are, and feel that we are important in life. Our society is afflicted with the illness of "not enough" and our teenagers are suffering the consequences of it. This type of thinking undermines the growth of healthy self-esteem. It sets up a pattern of dissatisfaction with self because the underlying message is "I am not enough."

We are enough, and it is our job as educators and parents to help our children feel safe and secure in who they are. We can help teenagers build their self-esteem by guiding them to concentrate on skills on talents they have instead of longing to be someone else. Assist them to clarify goals and to visualize themselves as successful in whatever they want to do.

The clearer the picture, the better the chance they have of building a positive self-image. "Accepting Myself" is an excellent imagery to build self-esteem and healthy attitudes that will shape the direction of a teenager's life.

The Journey

Close your eyes and focus your attention on your breath. As you breathe in... and out... gently through your nose or mouth, allow yourself to become more and more relaxed. As you gently breathe in... and ... out, your feet become relaxed..., your legs, become relaxed..., your abdomen becomes relaxed..., your back and shoulders become relaxed..., and your arms and hands become relaxed.... And as you continue to breathe in... and... out, gently and quietly, your head becomes relaxed and your mind floats free.

You find yourself floating away from this room to a place where you feel really good. It may be a place in nature, a place you have visited on vacation, anywhere where you feel good about yourself.

When you get there, just enjoy being there. Enjoy the warmth of the sun... and breathe it into yourself. Feel the warmth of the sun and feel filled with love. Now see yourself as perfect exactly the way you are... as a friend... with your family... with yourself. See yourself at ease with something that you enjoy doing, whether it is soccer, ice-skating, playing piano, drawing, singing, conversing with friends, or being alone. Just experience the joy of being you.

Pause

Continue to feel the warmth of the sun and to breathe in a feeling of peace and well-being.

Pause

Now I am going to call you back. Bring this feeling of well-being with you, and carry it with you throughout the day. I will count to three. Open your eyes at the count of three, ready to draw or write about your experience. One... two... three.

Maureen Murdock is an educator, therapist, and artist. She discovered the benefits of guided imagery with her own children and then took these techniques into her classroom and therapy practice. She has conducted workshops across the United States and Canada for therapists, teachers, and parents.

56

Spacecraft

Guide: Margaret Holland, Ph.D.

"Guided imagery is a very successful strategy for helping children overcome their own negative expectations."

Introduction

This is a fun, exciting imagery that children can practice to gain a sense of self-control and independence. It puts them in charge and gives them responsibility for "piloting" their own crafts. It requires decision making and patience. Remember to give children the opportunity to process their experiences, through the use of drawings or written words. This helps youngsters capture the experience for themselves before they begin to share verbally with others. It is also important to assure children that there are no right or wrong experiences — just lessons and insight to be gained.

The Journey

For this experience, you discover you are a pilot of a spacecraft. You're sitting in your spacecraft on the ground on a planet somewhere in the galaxy. Your co-pilot is sitting beside you getting ready for your flight. You feel yourself resting in your reclining chair.

Notice the control panel in front of you and blinking lights of different instruments giving you information about your craft. You hear the sounds of the engine starting because you are almost ready for lift-off, and you're feeling calm yet excited knowing that you are about to take off again into space. Now the engine sounds are louder, and the lift off begins. You look around feeling ready, knowing that the computer will control your craft as you lift. And so the countdown goes... four, three, two, one... lift off. The engines surge, and you feel their thrust as they begin to gather power and lift upward off the launching pad. Notice that everything is going well. Now you feel the pull of the gravity. It is pushing on your body, and so your body tightens and tenses... tenses all over... tense, tense, tense. Now you feel the weight of the gravity pushing against you as the ship continues up and the gravity pushes harder against you. Suddenly you realize that you are beginning to leave the gravity field. All of your muscles let go and you feel the loose, limp, floaty feelings of weightlessness. You turn and smile at your co-pilot who smiles back. You are feeling happy now that you are again in space looking around, looking at the planet you are leaving, and feeling a sense of calm excitement as you set out as the captain of another space mission.

Your enjoyment is interrupted by a call from mission control telling you that a shower of meteors has been sighted above you, and your programmed controls are not responding. You will have to take control of the ship and guide it through this dangerous meteor shower. You flip the switch and take control, noticing that you feel clam and in charge, knowing that you can do this, that you can fly your ship through this dangerous period. Now you are maneuvering the ship, watching the screen, watching the meteors and feeling in charge knowing that you can do it. And now you are flying through them, knowing that in a moment you will have gotten all the way through this meteor shower. Now you are at the other side. You breathe out slowly, and smile. And your co-pilot turns to you, smiles at you, and tells you what a great job you have done and how well you have responded to this emergency situation.

You lean back putting the spaceship back on computer-programmed control, smiling to yourself, feeling calm and good and confident. You know that you handled this emergency situation well, and you appreciate the good feelings of being in control and handling a dangerous experience.

Now the image of the spacecraft gradually begins to disappear. And as the spacecraft disappears, you come back to now, and bring back with you the good feelings of confidence, knowing that you handled an emergency situation well. So wiggle your toes now and stretch and maybe yawn, and when you are ready, open your eyes and smile.

Margaret Holland, Ph.D., is a professor of education at the University of South Florida in Tampa and a yoga teacher. She has a Ph.D. in Interpersonal Communication. She has done research in the effects of stress on learning and has worked with college athletes to improve their performance through imagery rehearsal.

Grief

57

Confronting Death

Guide: Stephen Levine

*"When we take death within,
life becomes clear and workable."*

Introduction

Although the approach to life's end may indeed be difficult, painful, confusing, the end of this "end game" has a much different quality....

Death is the process of expansion. It is a progressive release from the dominance of the qualities that compose all substance.... The stages of dying are the stages of going from solidity to spaciousness. Each step of the process is one of greater expansiveness....

[Meditations such as this one are widely used by those who are dying and by those helping a loved one prepare for death.] And yet more important than preparing us for death is their capacity to focus us on life. To let go of the last moment and to open to the next is to die consciously, moment to moment.

The Journey

Find a comfortable place to sit and let your eyes close.... Bring your attention to the level of sensation.... Feel this body you sit in. Let the body be still.... Focus on the sensation of being in a body. Notice the body's substantial quality.... Feel the solidity of the body.... Feel its weightiness, how gravity pulls on its substance.... Receive this quality of solidity....

Feel the weight of the head resting on the neck. Feel the musculature of that neck, its strength, its thickness.... Feel the long bones of the shoulders and the thick bony sockets that support the weight of the arms.... Feel the heaviness of the arms as they rest on either side of the body.... Feel these heavy hands.... Feel the torso, its thickness, its weightiness.... The earthen quality of this body. Feel this heavy body in which you live.

Notice the solidity, the density, the earth element, of the dense body.... The pull of gravity as the buttocks are drawn into the cushion or the chair, as the feet press against the floor.... Notice gravity's action on this earthen body.

In this solid body, sensations arise. Tinglings, hot and cold, rough and smooth, soft and hard. Sensations arising in the body.... Recognize the flickering field of sensation.... Don't grasp at sensation. Just allow these sensations to be received as they arise in this body we inhabit.

Open to the sensations in the legs, their density, heaviness.... Feel the solidness of this body.... Explore this container for the life-force.... And explore the life-force as sensation arising and passing away.

And as you note these sensations, notice how though they arise in the heavy body, they seem to be received by something subtler within. Something lighter within this heavier form.... Within this heavy body is a body of awareness, a light body which experiences hearing, seeing, tasting, touching, smelling, received through the outer body.... Feel the body of awareness, this inner body, this light body, perfectly nestled within the heavier form, receiving experience — experiencing.

Sense the lighter body within. The body of awareness that experiences all that enters through the senses. It recognizes sound as hearing. It delights in music. It experiences images as seeing. And recognizes great beauty. It experiences food as taste.... It knows it is alive.

Enter this light body of awareness.

Observe how each breath drawn in though the nostrils of the heavy body is experienced as sensation by the light body, by the awareness within.... Notice how each breath connects the heavy body with the light body. Each breath maintaining the light body within.... Each breath allowing life, awareness, to remain in the earthen vessel

Observe the light body receiving the heavy body.... Feel this contact between the heavy body and the light body that each breath allows.... Feel how each breath sustains the light body balanced perfectly within. Breathe the connection between the outer body and the inner body drawn in as air, received as sensation.... Each breath so precious. Each breath maintaining the connection, allowing life to remain in the body.... Feel how the breath connects the solid body with the light body. Experience each breath.... Just awareness and sensation. Each breath. Experience this delicate balance, moment to moment, as sensation, as awareness itself.... And take each breath as though it were the last.... Experience each inhalation as though it were never to be followed by another.... Each breath the last.... The last breath of incarnation.... Let the breath come. Let the breath go.... The last breath of life leaving the heavy body behind.... Each breath ending. The connection severed between the heavy body and the light body.... The end of a lifetime. The final breath.... Each breath the last.

Let go. Don't hold on to it.... Let each breath go, finally and forever. Don't even be attached to the next breath.... As the last breath leaves go with it. Don't hold on let yourself die. Let the light body float free now.... Let yourself die.... Let go now.... Gently, gently, let it all go. Let it all float free. Let yourself die.

Leave the body behind and follow the light into luminous space.... Go into it. Let yourself die into space.... Each breath vanishes. Each thought dissolving into space. Don't hold now. Just let go once and for all. Let go of fear. Let go of longing. Open to the wonder.... Let yourself die. Open into death. Nothing to hold to. That is all past. Die gently into this moment.... Holding on to nothing, just let yourself die.

Let go of your name. Let go of your face. Let go of your reputation. Float free into the vastness.... Leave the body behind. Moving into the vast space of being.... Light dissolving into light. Just vast luminous space. Let go now. Have mercy on you, let yourself float free.... Merging with space. Space dissolving in space. Light dissolving in light.... Vast, boudaryless, space, expanding into space.... Such enormous peace.... Dissolving. Dissolving. Edges melting. Vast, luminous space, dissolving in space.... Shimmering clouds dissolving at the edge. Clouds dissolving in space. Dissipating.

Dissolving. Merging in space.... Let go into that spaciousness. Hold nowhere. Let your heart merge in your own great fire.... Dissolving. Radiating into space. Merging with light. Dissolving in luminous space.... Let go into the light. In this vast luminosity is all that you have ever sought. Dissolving into the Great Heart.

Let go completely. Die gently into the light.... Floating free in vast space.... Let go of your knowing. Let go of your not knowing. All that comes to mind is old. Any thought is just old thought. Nothing to hold to.... "Just the simple fact of dying and the fact of the clear light...." Just the light entering the light.... Space within space.... No inside, no outside. Just am-ness. Edgeless being in endless space.... Dissolve into it. Floating free of the body, free of the mind. Merging in boundaryless space.... Space expanding into space. Dissolving into space. Floating in the vastness.... Peace. Mercy. Space.

And from across vast space notice now something gently approaching. It is the first breath of life.... Watch the breath approaching as if from far away. Experience it entering the body.... Each breath the first. Each inhalation the first breath of life.... Each breath completely new.... Each breath brining us back into the body.... Taking birth once again.... Born back into the body.... Taking birth again to serve and be served. To learn. To teach. To care and be cared for.... Awareness once again entering the body as consciousness.... Pure awareness reinhabiting pure form. Birth.... Born again into the body. Each breath the first. Born again to bring mercy and healing to the injured world.... Taking birth for the benefit of all sentient beings.... Taking birth to heal.... The light body once again reanimating the heavy body. Each breath connecting, maintaining the light body within its momentary vehicle.... Once again the light clothes itself in form so as to act and to complete whatever healing remains.... Have mercy. Born again to the world. Born to bring peace, to bring kindness. To bring healing to our pain and the pain of all sentient beings, unto the last blade of grass.... Born to learn, to be.... Each breath so precious, allowing us to stay a moment longer. Allowing us the healing we took birth for.... Born to take the teaching. Born to bring mercy.

May all beings coming and going know the peace of their own great nature. May all beings be free of suffering.... Let your eyes gently open.... Look around you. Here you are.

In the mid-1970's, while working with Ram Dass (Grist for the Mill, *1976) Stephen Levine taught meditation in the California prison system. For the next few years he led workshops and learned from the terminally ill the need for deeper levels of healing and the profound joy of service* (A Gradual Awakening, *1979). In 1979 he began teaching workshops with his wife, Ondrea. As co-directors of the Hanuman Foundation Dying Project, as they continued to serve the terminally ill and those deeply affected by loss. Their guided meditations for healing grief, heavy emotional states, sexual abuse, and subtler forms of life/death preparation brought them international recognition* (Healing into Life and Death, *1987.)*

Past Lives

58

Great Temple

Guide: Janet Doucette

*"This is a way to connect our past issues
with present paths of purpose."*

Introduction

This journey is deeply moving and can be used to better
understand the great purpose of which our spirits are well
aware. By providing a small "snapshot" of the issues in our
former lives, we can weave those issues into what we are
learning presently. I encourage users of this journey to allow
about twenty minutes for the experience of the previous life
review. This meditation can be practiced regularly when you
have a need to "sort" out issues.

The Journey

Begin with mindful breathing. Sit straight with spine erect
and your hands placed gently upon your thighs. As you
breathe, allow the breath to spiral down through your body,
nourishing your cells and organs. Relax and with the exhale,
release the toxins and the tensions accumulated during the
day into a white light that surrounds you. Sense your chakra
energy centers opening one by one, spinning in a clockwise
fashion....

You are standing on a beach at twilight. The sun's last golden rays are spilling across a gentle sea. Waves ripple up the shore and bathe your feet in cool salt water. Begin now to walk down the beach, feeling a sense of freedom and acceptance. Feel the love of Mother Earth well up through your legs and the warmth of Father Sky shine down upon your head.

Pause

As the sun sinks into the sea in a fiery moment of splendor, a green flash bursts forth across the darkening heavens. A sign of earth healing, it spreads out across the land. The pale blue sky darkens into indigo and then a velvety black expanse. There is a sparkle high in the night sky, as the stars show themselves. Feeling confident, you continue on.

A huge yellow orb rises from the depths of the sea and casts an eery pale light across the waters and upon the beach. The moment of the moonrise over the dark rippling ocean is a sacred moment. The reflected light of the dying sun upon the wakening face of the Moon casts a crystal awareness onto the world. Carried on the undulating surface of the sea, it is cast across your path. Walk now into that sacred light and stand within it.

This is a world between illusions, a world of pale reality in which you now walk. See before you now a mist and within that mist a great, white Temple by the Sea. White marble steps lead up to tall alabaster columns. Look carefully at this Temple now.

Pause

Walk purposely toward the Temple and climb the steps. As

you walk upon the smooth marble platform, the great doors open. You are welcome here. Enter, now....

Beyond a fountain of water, in the center of the Temple, is an immense library. Go now into the library and look for your name among the leather bound books.

Open the book that bears your name and run your finger down the page. Look into this book in which is recorded all the lives that you have lived, and see a word or phrase of words that encompass one of those lives.

Pause

Remembering that word or words, leave the library now and go beyond the Fountain to the Hall of Memories. You are now going to view that past life which points the way to understanding your present life and path of purpose.

Pause

In the Hall of Memories you are led to an ornately crafted door. Open that door now and step out into that other lifetime.

Look at your feet, your body. What are you wearing? Are you male or female? Take a few moments to fully see your appearance.

Where are you? Note your surroundings and anyone who may be with you now.

You are now going to relive this life. Take as long as you wish to recover what you need to know from this Life.

Pause

See the manner in which you leave this Life, the manner in which you pass on to another dimension. A place of peace and rest, where you are fully accepted as your high spiritual self. See the way in which you have planned the lessons of your lives, the courage of your chosen path of existence as a revered student, beloved of the creator.

Pause

Know that you will enter this place when you leave the present life which you are now leading in the present time. Know that you are fully loved here and that your teacher is well pleased. Whatever appears to be a mistake in this life is also a path to learning. First you must learn patience with yourself and others. Then you must learn acceptance of self and others. When you are ready, through the careful Paths of Many Lives, you will learn to radiate the Love which you have learned. For when you have learned to truly love yourself, then only, can you truly love another.

When you are ready to leave the Great Temple, see that you are again upon that misty, pale beach. Walk out of the moonlit beam of light and onto the deserted stretch of sand. When you are ready to return, flex your wrists and ankles gently.... Welcome back.

Janet Ware Doucette, of Brewster, Massachusetts, uses guided imagery and cross-cultural healing techniques in workshops and support groups in order to enable others to experience their higher selves. A profound near-death experience in 1986 left her with an awareness of our abilities to heal ourselves.

Meditations On Tape

ORDER FORM

NAME_____

ADDRESS_____

CITY _____

STATE/ZIP _____

PHONE _____

AUDIO CASSETTES

❑ **Journeys of the Mind I**   **$10.00**
Larry Moen
Side 1: Mother • Body Breathing
Side 2: Window • Seed of Light

❑ **Journeys of the Mind II**   **$10.00**
Larry Moen
Side 1: Peaceful Void • Healing Stars
Side 2: Let Go Fear • Bedwetting

❑ **Journeys of the Mind III**   **$10.00**
Larry Moen
Side 1: Butterflies • Internal Mother
Side 2: Oneness • Soldier of Light

❑ **Meditation in the Real World**   **$10.00**
Mona O'Neal
Side 1: Health • Peace of Mind
Side 2: Relationships • Anger and Forgiveness

❑ **Reflections in the River**   **$12.00**
Annette Covatta
Side 1: The Stillness Within • Mountain Peaks
Side 2: Songs of the Sea • Winter Seeds
• Being At One With Earth

❑ **Creative Imagineering**   **$20.00**
Tom Kenyon, ABR
Brain Entertainment and Psychoacoustic Stimulation
To Increase Mental Imagery, Visualization & Intelligence

Shipping   **$2.90**

                                        TOTAL_____

MAKE CHECKS PAYABLE TO: United States Publishing
and return with order form to: United States Publishing
3485 Mercantile Avenue • Naples, Florida 33942